OVERCOMING

ADOLESCENCE

Smyth & Helwys Publishing, Inc.
6316 Peake Road
Macon, Georgia 31210-3960
1-800-747-3016
©2011 by Marion D. Aldridge
All rights reserved.
Printed in the United States of America.

The paper used in this publication meets the minimum requirements of
American National Standard for Information Sciences—
Permanence of Paper for Printed Library Materials.
ANSI Z39.48–1984. (alk. paper)

*Library of Congress Cataloging-in-Publication Data*

Aldridge, Marion D., 1947–
Overcoming adolescence : growing beyond childhood into maturity / by Marion D. Aldridge.
p. cm.
Includes bibliographical references.
ISBN 978-1-57312-577-2 (pbk. : alk. paper)
1. Adolescent psychology.
2. Teenagers—Conduct of life.
3. Developmental psychology.
4. Maturation (Psychology)
5. Psychology, Religious.
I. Title.
BF724.A37 2011
155.5—dc22

2011004707

# OVERCOMING
## *adolescence*

### GROWING BEYOND CHILDHOOD
### INTO MATURITY

Marion D. Aldridge

# Also by Marion D. Aldridge

*The Pastor's Guidebook: A Manual for Worship*

*The Pastor's Guidebook: A Manual for Special Occasions*

*The Changing Shape of Protestantism in the South*
(edited with Kevin Lewis)

# Dedication

To the Four Life Guides
who helped me grow from being a pretend adult
to an authentic adult—

Sally Aldridge
Fuzzy Thompson
Randy Wright
Paul Carlson

and
To Ted Godfrey and Marcia Vernberg
for their great gifts of
Time and Space

# Contents

# Chapter 1

# Blind Date

Issue: *Process*

Objective: I will implement positive changes.

You don't know me and I don't know you, so this is something like a blind date. For some mysterious reason, we have ended up together. I have a story to tell. Of course, you also have a story—many stories, in fact. I will postpone telling you the entire narrative of my existence, especially my most foolish mistakes, until you know me a bit better.

If we proceed too quickly with too much about me, including even a few of my defects and deficiencies, you could write me off in the first ten minutes of this literary relationship, as people have done on many actual blind dates. Why should you rendezvous with a person or read a book written by someone with a history like mine? I prefer to ease into this liaison.

I have successes and failures in my past. You can probably learn something from my victories and my mistakes. Eventually, I will tell you some of each. I am neither a total hero nor a complete idiot, yet I have moments as both.

Here are a few ingredients in the stew that is my story:

I am Marion Douglas Aldridge. Each name means something. I am at least partly named after Francis Marion, the "Swamp Fox," a Revolutionary War hero from South Carolina. I am also named after two uncles called Douglas, one from each side of the family.

I am the second child (and the second son) of Allene Hipps and Carlton Aldridge. I am the brother of Edmund, the husband of Sally, the father of Jenna and Julie, the father-in-law of Thorne and Tom, and the grandfather of Lake. I love my family and am deeply committed to them.

My addiction of choice is warm pastry.

I was born in 1947 in Savannah, Georgia, on a cold February morning. We moved up the Savannah River to Augusta, Georgia, for a few years, then, during elementary school, across the river to South Carolina. I have lived most of my life as a proud South Carolinian.

My dad said our heritage consists of "Scotch, Irish, Dutch, and Devil."

We (my family, my neighbors, and everyone I knew) were racists.

I was born into the Christian faith, and I remain a Christian by choice.

I was raised a Southern Baptist, but I am no longer a Southern Baptist by choice.

My career path (so far) has had three major incarnations, first as a youth worker, then as a pastor, and now as a denominational executive.

Around age sixteen to eighteen, along with most other teenagers, I felt I had reached an intellectual zenith of some sort. In my own arrogant estimation, I thought it would be hard for me to get much brighter or more perceptive than I was when I graduated from high school. I had scaled and attained a peak of conceit. Adolescence is when most people quit learning. Teenagers know everything. Formal education is no longer required.

Then, with no effort at all, some teens turn into adolescent adults! They sign on (by default) for permanent immaturity. They never overcome adolescence.

Some people are humble enough to continue to ask for help along the way. They acquire information on how to perform a new job, how to cook, how to invest, how to breastfeed, or how to lose weight; but an alarming number of adults never learn much of anything from adolescence onward. They are permanently stuck, emotionally and intellectually, in their childhood and youth. They entertain few new thoughts and attempt to learn few new skills for the remainder of their lives.

Over the past thirty years, beginning at about age thirty, I have recognized that some of my lifelong habits and patterns needed to be radically altered. I discovered ways to make those adjustments. I am not the person I once was. Some of the modifications I made in old habits were painful. Change usually produces emotional discomfort somewhere in the process. Transformation is almost always troublesome.

I have three goals for this volume:

1. To provide encouragement and motivation to fellow travelers who are ready to make important decisions about living differently.

2. To provide insights and information about how to achieve and maintain a rich and rewarding life in which family, work, spiritual, social, intellectual, and emotional relationships are healthy and satisfying.

3. To provide practical tools and techniques to help individuals make the changes they want to make.

## Motivation + Insight + Action = Positive Change

We all need help. Your parents, or their substitutes, may have given you a good beginning, but maybe they didn't. Maybe they were effective and helpful only up to a point. Your church, synagogue, mosque, or school may have been supportive, but maybe not. Maybe they were beneficial only up to a point. Your current family, friends, and organizational affiliations may be just right for you, but maybe not. People will not change for the better without new insights and motivation coming from somewhere—from a coach, boss, spouse, parent, mentor, therapist, pastor, priest, rabbi, teacher, guide, counselor, stranger, or even a book. This volume ultimately cannot replace living human feedback, but perhaps it can help you get started.

> "There is a child within us . . . we must persuade not to be afraid."
>
> —PLATO, THE TRIAL AND DEATH OF SOCRATES

No one is born able to hit the bull's-eye with the first arrow and with every shot thereafter. Practice is required to get it right, to hit the mark. Feedback and accountability are necessary. Without paying attention to results, we don't know whether we are hitting the bull's-eye or striking the ground twenty feet from the target.

On this blind date of ours, I'm ready to give you a brief analysis of four areas where I overcame adolescent beliefs, models, and habits:

1. Eating as much as I wanted with impunity. Skinny, hyperactive teenage boys simply do not gain weight. Middle-aged and older guys do!

2. Clueless irresponsibility with regard to money. I was utterly unprepared for the adult realities of credit cards, taxes, and mortgages.

3. The naïve belief that perfection is possible. I assumed that if both parties in a conflict simply did the "right thing," then their problem would resolve. Better yet, I figured it was best never to disagree in the first place!

4. The foolish assumption that the career my teenage self chose for me was the appropriate vocation for my life.

In each area, hard data validates that I underwent a reformation regarding my lifestyle and habits. I will tell a few of my stories in the hope that you will soon tell your own tales of transformation.

## Losing Weight Permanently

A couple of years ago, during my annual physical examination, my doctor made me mad. In addition to the cholesterol medicine I was already taking, he prescribed a second pill for lowering my cholesterol, then a third because I had high blood pressure. When I whined that sweets were my problem, he said, "Then see a psychiatrist."

He made his point. He couldn't help me get me well if I continued doing everything I could to stay unwell. He couldn't fix me if I was determined to stay broken. He couldn't heal me if I continued to eat and act unhealthily.

"Think of sweets as poison," he warned.

I got serious about losing weight. I had never been a dieter. My weight did not fluctuate up and down. My weight simply went up. I am 5' 8" tall and I finally peaked at 217 pounds. Medical journals call that obese. Sometimes they call it morbidly obese.

To lose weight, I chose the same methodology I had used in dealing with other bad habits and addictions. I began by setting a realistic goal. I kept a journal that provided encouragement, motivation, and accountability. I joined Weight Watchers. I attempted to understand if there were deeper issues other than simply my enjoyment of tasty foods. A half-year into the project, I heard myself saying to one of my daughters the exact words my parents had uttered to me a million times: "Be sweet." My belly, my words, and my habits were drenched in honey and covered with chocolate.

There is usually more to our habits than we might suspect. Human existence is rarely simple. Successfully changing long-term behavior requires multiple and enduring efforts. Maybe some people can move swiftly and easily from one lifelong habit to another, but I can't. I have heard some religious converts say that after their "conversion," change came easily. I have heard others say they had to fight the same old battles and demons every single day. I am in the latter group. For me to change permanently in any area, I need constant motivation. Hearing and reading helpful, practical advice benefits me. The success of Weight Watchers, Alcoholics Anonymous, and other "self-help" groups is not limited to *self*-help. It always involves huge doses of feedback, suggestions, encouragement, and advice from others.

Everyone who has ever attempted to shed pounds knows about yo-yo dieting. Long-term change involves more than discipline and character. There is always a bigger picture. In order to eat right, you need to shop right. If you are going to shop right, you need to plan your shopping wisely. Every good diet plan recommends not shopping while you are hungry, making lists before going to the grocery store, and learning to read labels. Any time we intend to change, we had better be prepared to work, to think, and to make an effort. Simply wishing for change rarely brings results.

As I write this book, my weight has consistently remained twenty-two to twenty-eight pounds below my peak weight for more than five years. I may surprise myself, but I don't think I will ever regain all of those pounds.

## Succeeding Financially

After the first phase of my own therapy thirty years ago, I was able to name some of the issues that had haunted and limited me. A good therapist, coach, mentor, or friend can help you do that. Sometimes a boss, a parent, a spouse, or even a child can tell us exactly what our problems are, but we don't always value their opinions!

One of my realities was a life script that told me to "be poor." Other related family scripts played into this theme. I was raised in a Christian home and attempting to "be Christian" (another life script). In the Bible, Jesus tells a young man to sell all he has and give it to the poor (Matt 19:21). With that clear instruction, I wondered how a person could be wealthy and Christian at the same time. My parents were lower middle class, and they seemed to doubt the sincerity of the few members of our small, blue-collar church who lived in our town's nicer neighborhoods. To our family, money was somehow tainted or evil. As a young adult, I was semi-proud of the fact that I had never once read the financial pages of the newspaper.

> "We are defined by what we fear."
>
> —GORDON LIVINGSTON, *AND NEVER STOP DANCING*

As my therapist, Paul Carlson, began to challenge me to alter certain family scripts, he recommended that I rewrite this one. I began to pay attention to various viewpoints on the subject of economic well-being that championed an alternative philosophy. Ideas like these motivated me to develop a new perspective toward money:

• "With money in your pocket, you are wise and you are handsome and you sing well too." (Yiddish proverb)
• "When God gives people wealth and possessions and enables them to enjoy and accept their lot, and to be happy in their work, this is a gift of God." (Ecclesiastes 5:19)
• "Gain all you can; save all you can; give all you can." (John Wesley)
• "Go into the street and give one man a lecture on morality and another a shilling, and see which will respect you the most." (Samuel Johnson)

There are hundreds more proverbs like these, and, of course, there are count-less cautionary adages about accumulating and hoarding wealth. When I began this process as a young man, my problem was not greed or avarice. My problem with regard to money, as in so many other areas, was an incomplete adolescent worldview that I needed to overcome. A misguided notion from childhood about the evils of money dominated my understanding of eco-nomics. What I believed to be absolutely and completely true turned out to be only a portion of the truth. I discovered that money, rather than being evil, was morally neutral. We can achieve good or bad with it. We can con-trol capital, or capital can control us.

An important part of my strategy to change involved what I called "action goals." In each area where I wanted to be different, I set small goals that would move me in a new direction. My therapist repeatedly reminded me, "You act your way to a new set of feelings. You do not feel your way to a new set of actions." In this instance, I set several goals, including investing in the stock market, buying property (real estate), enjoying one nice trip (at least) each year, and "dressing for success."

I did all of the above, but the most exciting goal has been my decision to take a trip each year. Since age thirty-five, I have traveled extensively. More than a quarter of a century has passed, and I have not missed a single year of taking a fantastic excursion. I have been to more than two dozen countries in North, Central, and South America, Europe, Asia, and Africa.

I changed. I made a decision, developed a strategy, and have been func-tioning in a different way than I once did. It is not an incidental fact that I have done this with no debt other than the modest and appropriate use of a credit card required for international travel.

I am no longer controlled by a mindless ethic that believes poverty, in and of itself, is a holy and desirable state. I have grown beyond the confine-ments of my childhood.

# Mending Broken Relationships

Every day someone exasperates me in a new way: my wife, one of my children, my grandson, a friend, a cab driver, a colleague, a waitress, the governor, the president. Unless you are a hermit, you must relate to other people. Who doesn't want romance, a true friend, a partner, a companion, a meaningful job, an ally, camaraderie, intimacy, and fellowship?

But relationships are hard!

In any list of reasons that people are unhappy, relationships of various kinds are almost always near the top of the list, immediately following issues of life and death (food, water, shelter, warmth). I entered therapy, initially, as a result of my disappointment in several relationships. I had been married long enough to discover that my wife was not perfect. If she were, she would always understand me and my point of view and agree with it, yet sometimes she was mad at me. By the time I got around to therapy, I was able to admit that she also made me mad! Indeed, one of the first things I learned from my counselor was to name my own demons appropriately. Mature adults, I thought, were not supposed to get angry. I would piously (and incorrectly) say I was "disappointed" in someone or "sad" about what they did. That was part of my self-righteous façade. Usually, I felt that I was guilty of nothing. I was not having affairs. I was not stealing money. I had murdered no one. I didn't beat my wife. Meanwhile, I stewed inside, pouting, sulking, whining, and complaining to anyone who would listen. I was Mr. Sarcasm. But mad? Of course not. I thought I was going to therapy to deal with people who were dissatisfied with me, but it did not take long for me to realize that my number-one priority (and the only thing I could control) was my anger and attitude toward others.

Specifically, our church's deacons were driving me crazy. These men (and they were all men) were supposed to be the most mature, responsible members of our church, men who would work with me and mentor me. I was thirty years old. Yet some of these older men were even more childish, petty, silly, and narcissistic than I was.

How do you fix broken relationships? That was the question. Initially, I did not see myself as the problem in any of the difficult circumstances I faced. The problem, I thought, was always the other person. At work, I quickly developed a good guys/bad guys dichotomy. All the people who supported me, my decisions, my leadership, and my opinions were the good guys. I could define irresponsible behavior in a variety of ways, but probably the most essential issue was whether or not a person agreed with me. If they were antagonistic toward me, then I saw them as irresponsible.

You do not need to be religious to be as self-righteous as I was. There are Hindus, Muslims, Buddhists, Christians, Jews, Secular Humanists, Pagans, Intellectual Elite, Democrats, Republicans, and others who are utterly certain of their own rightness. Pride, hubris, and arrogance are far more about your personality than your theology or your religion. You might also say of people who share this conceit that they are stubborn, obstinate, or inflexible.

Mature people have come to terms with the flaws in the fabric of the world. People cannot and will not mature until they are able to admit and even embrace the blemished nature of whatever is important to them: their parents, their religion, their country, their favorite sports team, their political party, their spouse, their siblings. Adversity happens. In therapy, I learned that lasting relationships require grace, tolerance, patience, charity, and unmerited benevolence. Using the document of my own faith tradition (the Bible), I began to understand that failure is a universal condition. No one is exempt. If I were going to get along in the world, I needed grace for other people, grace for myself, and grace from other people. No matter how much you or I may fantasize about the perfect marriage, the perfect job, perfect children, or perfect friends who will never disappoint us, they do not exist. Happy marriages, loyal friends, and fulfilling jobs are available, but perfection is not attainable by you, by me, or by anyone else. Every major religion says something to the effect that the happy or content person is not the one who gets everything she or he desires, but the person who finds what is available to be acceptable and satisfactory.

"To see what is right, and not to do it, is lack of courage."

—CONFUCIUS

The irony of relationships is that when I began to expect less, I began to value what I received more. In one instance, this became as clear to me as if a light bulb had been turned on over my head. While counseling two of the most brilliant people I had ever met, I suddenly realized that on a scale of 1 to 10, this couple had only two numbers, 0 and 10. No one qualified as a 6, 7, 8, or 9. They believed all of their professional colleagues were fools. Zeroes. Their children were failures. Their marriage partner was a disaster. They spent a lot of time being disgusted. There was no room in their relationships for "slightly irritating," "adequate," "okay," "sufficient," or "better than average." For them, everything was either perfect success or abject failure. In spite of the best Ivy League educations, they couldn't keep jobs, and they struggled with friendships over an extended period. They had no idea of the value of expecting less from other human beings.

As for hard data to verify whether I have remained in positive, intimate relationships, here are my statistics:

1. As I write this, I have remained happily married to my wife for thirty-seven years. We love each other more now than we did on our wedding day (when we were more in lust than in love). Over the years, we have had to learn to love each other, which means persevering through the tough times. Whatever love is, it is not so much what you feel when all is well in the relationship. Love is what you do when life is difficult.

2. I have two magnificent adult daughters, and I am not estranged from either one. Each of them makes me proud every day of my life. We get along and enjoy being together.

3. I have known my best friends for an average of forty years each. That doesn't mean I don't make new friends, but it does mean that my best buddies and I have hung together through divorces, depressions, job changes, bad health, and all kinds of other odious trials.

4. My jobs, throughout my career, have lasted an average of ten years each.

I mention these "statistics" because, otherwise, reliable, concrete data is difficult to come by in analyzing relationships. Regardless of statistical verification, I know this: a good dose of grace is crucial for meaningful and sustained adult relationships.

## Changing Careers

Twenty years into a career I believed I had chosen for altruistic motives, I discovered that my motives were probably more complicated. In our Baptist tradition, we talk about God "calling" us into the ministry. Being a pastor is a "vocation," from the Latin word "*vocare*," which means "to call," the same root from which we get the word "vocal." When you think you have heard God's voice, that is a big deal. Occasionally, I have met someone who believes they heard God's actual, literal voice, but that has never been my experience. Like most other pastors, I felt inner stirrings and promptings that led me, step by inevitable step, toward the profession of being a minister.

I was reasonably good, but not great, at what I did during my twenty-five-year career as a pastor. I helped a lot of people, but also I made a lot of people mad. It is an odd system: my salary came from people whom I needed to offend occasionally. People of all faiths have persecuted their prophets and have generally been annoyed by anyone who challenged the status quo of their culture. Yet challenging the status quo is what a good preacher or prophet or rabbi does, unless he or she intends to be the court chaplain. I have heard people say they like "to have their toes stepped on," but when the sermon spoke against racism, war, and greed, congregations were far less likely to listen patiently. My experience is that they rose up and attempted to do harm in one way or another to the messenger!

At the last church I pastored, eighty-two people signed a petition against me. I had considered some of them my friends. They made up about 10 percent of the congregation. I had worked in that church for fourteen years and, over the course of time, had offended many people in a variety of ways. As a lifelong people pleaser, this was an extremely stressful job for me. When people ask now about my life in the ministry, I speak fondly of my first few years out of college when I worked for a fine organization called Young Life. I also speak enthusiastically about my work now as the first state coordinator in South Carolina of a new organization that has grown ten times its original size in fewer than ten years, the Cooperative Baptist Fellowship. But I find myself describing my twenty-five years as a local church pastor as time spent in a black hole. I work as hard now as the CBF coordinator as I did as a pastor—with one-tenth of the stress. I love what I am doing now. I did not enjoy my career as a pastor. (Others, of course, are magnificent at the pastoral vocation. Remember that this is my story.)

Why did I remain a pastor for so long when I was equally qualified for fifty other professions that would have been more pleasurable and remunerative? As people begin a process of transformation, they have certain boundaries they will instinctively not transgress. They will not change religions. They will not get a divorce. They will not move away from their parents. They will not "waste" a college degree by changing jobs. They will not see a psychiatrist. These taboos differ for each person. Some of these prohibitions need to be examined and challenged.

One of the interesting quotations I came across was described as McCabe's Law, a corollary to Murphy's Law. McCabe's Law contends, "Nobody *has* to do anything." That is true.

"I've got to go by my mother's tonight," or "I must finish this project before our guests get here," are not accurate statements. Even if death results because you do not do something, it is not required that you do that task. There are duties we probably ought to do, but we always have options.

Even though I had two degrees from seminary (including a doctorate) and a good bit of experience in just one profession—not to mention that I was getting older by the day—I still had alternate career choices. People leave the ministry every day, just as people enter the ministry every day, at all ages and stages of life. Sometimes the career move is radical. Former ministers start selling insurance, go to work in a print shop, or return to the family farm. Sometimes the career move is seamless, as mine turned out to be. Before I took my current job, I considered a variety of options in the not-for-profit sector—working for a local food bank, the Heart Association, the Red Cross, etc. By the way, the budget of my organization the year before I became their first coordinator was not enough to pay my salary, much less benefits. So I did not fall into a cushy and comfortable job with this career change. There was risk involved. There still is. I still anger traditionalists and others, even in our progressive organization. Who knows whom I will irritate next, about what issue, and when.

> "Pooh, you're nothing but a pack of cards. I'm not afraid of you."
>
> —ALICE, TO THE QUEEN OF HEARTS, *ALICE IN WONDERLAND*

The question remains: "What factors changed the equation enough for me to take the plunge and risk a new career?" I could have continued as a pastor. The hostile ten percent of people in my church was not an insurmountable obstacle. Ten percent is, after all, a minority. Besides, most of those people had been antagonistic for fourteen years. In fact, I stayed on another year as pastor before taking the job I have now. One of the factors in my decision to change careers was a document someone gave me titled "Seven False Calls into the Ministry." As I read this paper, one of the "false calls" might as well have displayed my picture and biography beside it. The document assured its readers that any of these avenues of entering the ministry might later be validated as leading to a genuine vocation. For instance, some people entered the ministry because their mother set them on that career path. Son number 1 was to enter the ministry. Son number 2 was to become a doctor. Son number 3 was to be a lawyer. If they all did what Mama wanted, all three may be caught in what are possibly the wrong careers. Or they all three may be perfectly content in what they are doing.

My issue was power! I aspired to be powerful, though I never would have articulated that desire before I turned thirty years old. In my world, the most powerful person was "Preacher Smith," pastor of Immanuel Baptist Church in North Augusta, South Carolina. My family was blue collar, and we did not know the merchants in town. We did not know anyone who owned a business. We did not know the mayor or a single city or county councilman. We did not know any plant manager, police chief, hospital administrator, or white-collar executive. This church and its leader, the pastor, were the focal points of conversation at our dinner table. "The preacher said thus and so," we'd comment, or "The preacher's getting together a group to go to such and such a place." That was my life, and other than my parents, Preacher Smith (certainly not Elvis) was the king.

Don't misunderstand. This was not a megachurch whose pastor had a huge ego. Reverend Joseph W. Smith was a good man who led an average-sized, middle-class Baptist congregation. But my family and I admired him enough that I felt the ministry was the route to go if I were to amount to something significant. Of course, at the time I didn't understand my motivations. The document about "Seven False Calls," which a friend gave me after I completed seminary and had served for ten years as a pastor, was a wake-up call. My ministry was not invalidated, but at least I became less naïve about the genesis of my professional choice. Many of us do what we do for unintentional reasons. Some of those reasons may involve a true vocation. My wife teaches middle schoolers, and she has done so magnificently for more than forty years. She is clearly called to this profession. Part of her motivation for teaching related to a bad experience in her childhood with a lazy and incompetent middle school teacher.

If you know how you got to where you are in your career, then you can affirm it, or you can challenge and change it. If you are unhappy in your job, then you might need to separate yourself from the casual drift of your childhood, adolescent, or young adult choices. Maybe you need to grow up and make an adult decision about your vocation.

I finally did, and I am glad.

# Chapter 2

# Defined by What We Fear

Issue: *Courage*

Objectives: I will learn to feel safe within myself.
I will see myself as equal to others.

When I was a kid, my mother would send me to get a loaf of bread at the hovel not far from our house that doubled as a country store. The walk there and back was ten minutes of pure terror. We lived on the last street of the last subdivision in our small town, backed up to the pine woods that are typical of the South Carolina sand hills. The forest itself was friendly space. My brother, my buddies, and I built forts in the shallow, red-clay gullies and created baseball fields in the meadows. We climbed the trees. My big brother and I picked wild blueberries, blackberries, and plums there, and Mother made us cobblers from the fruit. We discovered an old moonshiner's still. On the other side of the narrow strip of woods was a country road that led to Beverly's Grocery Store, a small local market where we could purchase milk, bread, candy, and baseball cards. The distance between where I emerged from the path in the woods to Beverley's Grocery was no more than 100 yards, but no condemned prisoner ever felt more like a dead man walking than I did as I passed through a gauntlet of savage, growling, snarling dogs. There were anywhere from six to twelve of the beasts. I don't recall being bitten, but that never lessened my fear. I hated that short hike.

Though I am now an adult, I still despise barking, menacing, aggressive dogs. Why was I so fearful? Why am I still so apprehensive? While I am consciously aware of the spontaneous fright that pops up in me when I see an attacking dog rushing toward me, I am far more likely now to challenge the animal, at least to throw a rock at him. If I know I will meet a dog on a regular walking route, I carry a stick with me. When I told a friend about these episodes from when I was a boy, he said simply he would have shot the dogs. Where did my fear come from? Why did I feel so powerless against the dogs?

We are all afraid of something. We should be. We would likely not survive childhood without an appropriate sense of fear. There are different levels of fear.

Level 1 includes real, life-threatening situations: a drunk in a bar with a loaded gun, stampeding elephants, live exposed electrical wires, a hurricane bearing down on your community. Level 1 threats can kill, and adults should know when they are facing this type of risk. Small children, however, might think the rogue elephant is funny and laugh at it. Teenagers do not always recognize level 1 circumstances as critical. When they respond foolishly, for example, running toward trouble instead of in the opposite direction, we ask, "What were they thinking?" The answer is that they were not thinking. David Walsh, in his best-selling volume, *Why Do They Act That Way? A Survival Guide to the Adolescent Brain for You and Your Teen*, explains that the adolescent brain is not yet fully developed. Teens make choices (or fail to make choices) because they (a) lack adequate life experience and (b) lack fully developed brains! Adults, however, should recognize grave situations as serious. Healthy, appropriate fear is one sign of maturity.

Level 2 involves bosses who harass, neighbors who aggravate, and bullies who threaten. The fearful make an error when they elevate level 2 to level 1 with phrases such as, "That will just *kill* my mother" or "I was scared to *death*." As a wise friend once told me, "The only thing that is the end of the world is the end of the world." Disappointments are disappointing, but they are not deadly. Unhappy events make you unhappy. They don't make you dead! Those dogs on the way to Beverly's Grocery were a level 2 threat. Dogs can kill, but these were barking dogs, nuisances, not trained attack dogs. A sign of maturity, as opposed to adolescence, is recognizing the proper weight to give to a potentially threatening situation. Are you willing to lose your job today because you are unwilling to lose a meaningless argument? Maybe your boss is acting like a spoiled child, but do you need to act like a brat having a tantrum, too? Proportionate response is a sign of emotional health and maturity.

> "Victory is not won in miles, but in inches. Win a little now, hold your ground, and later win a little more."
>
> —LOUIS L'AMOUR

Level 3 is when people respond with alarm to non-threatening phenomena: black cats, elevators, ladders, the opinions of strangers. Mental health professionals have documented hundreds of phobias. Some people's reactions turn a level 3 situation into a level 1 emergency. When she sees a harmless spider, a woman jumps, knocking over a candle and starting a deadly fire. A competent driver waits at a stop sign, ready to accelerate onto a busy highway. Someone behind him honks. Growing anxious, the man in front pulls into a busy intersection and causes a wreck. But the honker's leg isn't broken. His insurance doesn't escalate. His wife isn't widowed. Why would people fear someone or something that can't actually harm them? Every day, people are terrorized for all the wrong reasons.

When we are young, our parents, teachers, and culture use fear to teach us right from wrong. If we do the wrong thing, we will face dreadful consequences. If we do the right thing, we will enjoy pleasant results. Whether through corporal punishment (as in my home) or social disapproval (sitting in the "time out" corner), the authority figures in our lives attempt to protect us from ourselves and from others. Fear is often a better motivator than logic, especially with children.

A certain level of fear is not necessarily bad. The problem is that too many adults still function like children with regard to fear. It is okay for a child to be concerned about what other people think, especially parents, grandparents, teachers, police officers, or other responsible adults. One of the first moral dilemmas a young person encounters is when to ignore an adult. We tell our sons and daughters to do that when a stranger offers them candy to get in a car. But in almost every other circumstance, we expect children to be submissive to adults.

We are not children. The greatest challenge of maturity is overcoming adolescence, and for some of us, it lasts far beyond our teenage years. One of the tasks of growing up is learning to make nuanced adult distinctions.

My pilgrimage toward better mental health began thirty years ago when I attended a weeklong continuing education event. Little did I realize that my life was about to change significantly and permanently. My typical pattern for such conferences was to carry several books, to sit on the back row, and, if the speaker did not engage me, to catch up on my reading.

On this occasion, the conference participants were randomly divided into small groups of eight to ten people, each with two leaders. After giving initial detailed introductions about ourselves and our work environments, we were asked to talk about the demanding emotional issues that concerned us regarding our job performance. This was not what I had bargained for! It was too personal. Furthermore, I could hardly read in a small group when I was supposed to be a sensitive participant deeply concerned about the problems of my peers. We were to meet together in this configuration for almost a week. Some of my colleagues packed up and left within twenty-four hours.

Those who remained sat there staring at the tops of our shoes. After a period of general discomfort by everyone in the group, I dove in, heedless about what rock lay hidden just beneath the water. I reasoned that I was there to learn and grow, and maybe I could improve on my unhappiness with my first pastorate. None of my deacons was present. I was one of the youngest in the group. I figured, why not get free advice and sympathy from these experienced people. I was skilled at describing my side of a conflict. I thought these men would listen, com-

> "Success is the result of making many mistakes and learning from experience."
>
> —WINSTON CHURCHILL

miserate, agree that my plight was difficult, and give me a bit of shrewd counsel. Then we would move on to the next person, and I could relax and enjoy the rest of our days together.

It didn't work out that way.

I said my spiel, and, sure enough, my elder colleagues' words of wisdom, compassion, and approval inundated me. They seemed to believe I had made all the right choices. According to them, I had said and done the appropriate things in the early crises of my career. There appeared to be a general consensus that I would go far in my profession. Way to go, me! So far, so good.

Then one of the group leaders broke the congratulatory mood. He asked me if there was anyone in the group I didn't like. In our polite Southern culture, I was not accustomed to such blunt questions, but instantly I decided that if he was insensitive enough to ask the question, I would be tactless enough to answer it.

"You," I responded.

"Okay," he said, and he didn't seem defensive. He asked a follow-up question, as if my reply had not surprised him.

"Do I remind you of anyone you work with?"

"Yes."

He asked me to name my adversary, and I did. I don't recall the exact words in the series of additional questions he asked, but, one by one, he led me back through my employment and associations of the past ten years, each time asking me if there was someone in my previous job with whom I had a similar contentious relationship. The answer was always "yes," and I had no trouble calling each person by name. These questions came quickly enough that I had no time to consider where he was leading me, or what the punch line would be. I simply went with the flow.

After only a few minutes had elapsed, he asked if I had these negative, even hostile feelings about anyone in the home in which I grew up.

I knew the answer, but I could not say it. I was crying. I was a thirty-three-year-old man who had not shed a tear since I was a teenager, yet I was incapable of speaking. I sobbed in front of the colleagues whom I had successfully impressed a few minutes earlier. Another minute passed before I was finally able to verbalize a response to his question.

"My brother." I wept some more before I finally added, "He used to beat me up."

Where had all that blubbering come from?

My only sibling, Edmund, two years older, did indeed "beat me up" when we were kids. I thought that was the prerogative of big brothers. Physically larger, a six-year-old boy is stronger than a four-year-old and uses his size to his advantage. That's what big brothers do—beat up little brothers. Why was I crying about it now? It was a long time ago. Edmund and I quit fighting, as most kids do, in our preteen years. Even those were twenty years earlier. As an adult, I have talked to my parents and to Edmund about this, and we all agree that Edmund was not a bully. Edmund was and is a fine person who just happened to be my big brother, taking advantage of the rights and privileges of being the stronger sibling. As adults, Edmund and I get along well, love each other deeply, and enjoy spending time together.

What transpired on this day at the conference came from deep inside an unexplored portion of my psyche. Obviously, there was a correlation between my relationship with my older brother and my antagonistic and often unpleasant relationships with the older, powerful men who later passed through my life (from my various bosses to the leader of this small group). Older, powerful males were a problem for me! I felt threatened by them and kept finding myself in hostile relationships with them.

Over the next few months and years, I began a quest of self-analysis. I participated in psychotherapy and became aware of ways my relationship with my brother had played itself out in my life. For instance, not wanting to engage in a fight I knew I would lose, I became a peacemaker. I always chose conversation over conflict, diplomacy over violence. I can tell myself that my predisposition to conciliation is the result of my religious faith, and maybe some of it is, but I suspect the fear of getting beat up is thrown into the mix.

Another pattern I noticed in my relationships was my tendency to fight easy targets that I could wound from a distance. Since I avoided direct defiance, I became expert at other forms of harassment. I became sarcastic. I wrote letters to the editor. I aimed my written arrows at people who had little or no power to strike back. I never confronted an individual directly. Instead, I talked to a third person, preferably someone who would agree with me. I did all the things children and adolescents do when they are unhappy with the world. I whined. I blamed. I felt sorry for myself.

Note the specific nature of my fear: *older, powerful males.* My mother was a standard-issue, nurturing mom, and I have never tended to be as uptight or fearful of strong, powerful women as I am of strong, powerful men. Of course, there are scary women who make my blood run cold and certain strong men who are also nurturing and put me at ease.

The point is that my emotions of fear and attitudes of anxiety are not universal, but are peculiar to me for reasons specific to my family and my life story.

Peter Steinke wrote, "Fear overwhelms us and actually diminishes our alertness. . . . The fearful person is barely able to focus on anything else. Tunnel vision occurs and fear takes over" ("Fear Factor," *Christian Century*, 20 February 2007). We live in a culture of fear. Yet most people would not think of themselves as fearful. I can't prove this, but I suspect that 90 percent of the problems most people have are the result of unnecessary fear:

- Fear of death
- Fear of disease
- Fear of failure
- Fear of being "found out"
- Fear of change
- Fear of crowds
- Fear of financial loss

- Fear of hell
- Fear of offending our parents
- Fear of physical pain
- Fear of public speaking
- Fear of the opinion of others
- Fear of the unknown

Substitute words such as "worry," "anxiety," "dread," or "shame" to reveal other fears. I can be worried that people will think I have bad breath, a bad marriage, a bad haircut, a substandard car or house, or that I eat at the wrong restaurant, wear the wrong clothes, et cetera. At least half the advertising on television appeals to our anxieties: if we don't buy a certain product, we will be ugly, we will be poor, we will have body odor, we will be shoddily dressed. Most political advertising is built on fear; if the other candidate is elected, our country and our world, as we have known it, will be gone forever.

Recently, I watched television for about ten minutes for the purpose of observing how advertisers play on our fears. Their primary tool for frightening us is embarrassment and shame: Will you regret . . . ? Are you paying too much . . . ? Are you plagued by unsightly, stubborn belly fat? Would you embarrass yourself by . . . ? Make your acne disappear . . . . Drink the wrong beer, and you won't be cool . . . . Are you worried about . . . ? Don't be humiliated by . . . . Don't let someone else get a better rate . . . .

In addition to fearing the "ailment" the particular product claims to cure, advertisers fabricate other ways to frighten us: You must act now! When the supply is gone . . . . If your orders don't go out, you lose money. If they don't arrive on time, you lose money. Seventy-two-hour sale! Hurry! Our product provides a certificate of authenticity. Don't be duped by competitors.

> "Habit is overcome by habit."
>
> —THOMAS À KEMPIS

The fabrication of fear, however, is not limited to television advertisers. Some sectors of society thrive on creating anxiety. Coaches couldn't function without the tool of fear. Teachers count on accountability (grades) to keep the majority of their students functioning normally. Bosses use different forms of fear. Apprehension and anxiety are seldom simple. These leaders can also be fearful that we will quit. We truly live in a culture built on fear.

Some anxieties are legitimate. It is an appropriate instinct to swat or duck when a wasp flies toward your eye. You should do your job to the best of your ability because you can be let go if you fail to meet your boss's standard. Snakes can bite you. Speeding cars driven by careless drivers wreck and maim and kill. Too much smoking, too much fatty food, and alcohol produce heart attacks. You should not put your hands inside the wild animal cages at the zoo.

But some social fears are misguided. Some people fear what other people think more than they fear getting certain illnesses or losing their jobs. Such social stigma produces a public purpose. If everyone simultaneously decided that it doesn't matter what other people think and thus quit their jobs, left their spouses, and abandoned their children, then we would have community chaos. Culture, society, and tradition conspire to keep you and me "in line" in order to prevent pandemonium. However, our lives are too often dominated by "shoulds" and "oughts" that make sense for children but may no longer apply to us as adults. My goal in saying, "Fear not," is not to create anarchy, but to have individuals do the right things at the right times for the right reasons.

One of my favorite quotations is often attributed to Brooke Astor, who reflects on the opinions others might have of her: "It was not until I was forty that I was able to go into a room and say to myself, 'What do I think of these people?' Before that, I had always thought, 'What do these people think of me?' When I became forty, I said to myself, 'You are either a whole person now or you never will be. Believe in yourself.'"

There is a distinction between getting advice about a specific course of action and needing someone's approval to act. There is a difference in being concerned about something and being continuously anxious. Life involves risks. Parenting involves risks. Being married involves risks. Being employed involves risks. Assessing the hazards that may result from a certain behavior is ordinary good sense. Fearing all mistakes is senseless. Some parents avoid disciplining their children for fear that the children will grow up with a problem that was caused by their discipline. Yet, raising undisciplined children is raising problem children. Even when they are adults chronologically, they will remain adolescents emotionally.

> "God grant me the serenity to accept the things I cannot change, courage to change the things I can, and wisdom to know the difference."
>
> —REINHOLD NIEBUHR

America was not built on fear. Healthy families are not built on fear. Adolescent angst may bind teenagers together briefly, but strong, permanent adult friendships are not built on fear. Someone said a mistake is only proof that someone was at least trying to accomplish something.

It is not merely coincidence that in the Hebrew Bible and in the New Testament, the Hebrew prophets, the angels, and Jesus are always saying, "Fear not." The mystics believed you could recognize an angel by their constant refrain, "Fear not."

# Chapter 3

# Pay Attention

Issue: Awareness

Objectives: I will learn the wisdom of listening, seeing, and paying attention. I will gain insight into the world and myself when I am alert to what is happening around me.

Not paying attention is a huge problem in Western culture. Here is my story.

Hans Christian Andersen wrote a fairy tale about the princess and the pea. The princess was so sensitive that even through a stack of twenty mattresses, she still felt the discomfort caused by that tiny pea. Her sensitivity proved she was a real princess, fit to marry the prince.

After I was married several years, I realized I had married a princess. Sitting in the same room, my wife, Sally, would complain of being cold, while I felt comfortable. That made sense. Some people are cold-natured. But, later, in another time and place, Sally would complain of being hot, while I still felt comfortable. Surely one can't be both cold-natured and hot-natured! Eventually, I remembered the story of the princess and the pea and concluded that my wife is ultra-sensitive. One might say she is "high maintenance." She has elevated expectations regarding her personal comfort. Even though twenty mattresses may separate her from that proverbial pea, she knows it's there, and she lets me know she feels it! Then she wants me to do something about that blasted pea, no matter how many mattresses I have to remove and replace.

So far, this sounds like a complaint about the princess's super-sensitivity, but it's not. Here's my part of the story. It's about the blue-collar kid and the cantaloupe. Instead of being extra sensitive like my wife, I tend to be less sensitive, even insensate, numb, anesthetized, and utterly unaware of the cantaloupe beneath my own thin mattress.

Sally and I would come home from somewhere and she would ask, "Do you smell that?"

"No," I would answer honestly. I sensed nothing.

Over time, too many episodes occurred when something was actually burning in the oven or making a noise that needed our attention. It wasn't just that I married a person with extra-keen perception; it was also that she married someone whose senses were apparently exceedingly dull. In trying to analyze what was going on, I have concluded that there were a couple reasons for my lack of awareness.

1. In the instance of not smelling, hearing, or seeing something, at least one aspect of my insensitivity was that I didn't want to encounter difficulty. If there were a problem—a commode overflowing, an electrical short in the light fixture, a noise in the ceiling fan, the smell of dog urine, twenty mattresses that needed to be restacked—I suspected it would fall on me to solve the crisis. Because I didn't want to face a problem, I at least subconsciously refused to see, hear, smell, taste, or feel one.

2. The more basic issue was that I had rarely ever listened, smelled, tasted, touched, saw, or felt with much consciousness or comprehension, and that insensitivity predated my relationship with Sally. Call it clueless. Call it naïve. Call it stupid. Call it immaturity. In the movie *Clueless* (Paramount Pictures, 1995), the teenage protagonist is hilarious. A fifty-year-old naïf is sad and frustrating.

Listening or paying attention was a challenge for me. It went hand in hand with my addiction to talking incessantly. My primary demon, which contributes to both of these defects, has to do with my fear of not being liked. I have heard it called "Approval Addiction."

In a prolonged, sometimes sluggish process, I have finally learned that, for a fully healthy human being, sensation is a gift. Not being able to feel is a curse. Seeing is a privilege, and not seeing is a nuisance; hearing is a capacity, and not hearing is an aggravation. God gave us five senses in order that we would pay attention by using them all.

The great sin of the Hebrew Scriptures is repeated over and over: "They would not listen!" (Jer 25:7) Roy Honeycutt, a Hebrew

> "Arrogance has a voice but no ears. Wisdom has a voice and listening ears."
>
> —REV. OTIS MOSS, JR.

scholar and the former president of the seminary I attended, said we usually translate the biblical prophets so that they are inoffensive. Our English Bible translations have God saying through the prophets (e.g., Isa 41:1), "Listen to me in silence." A more accurate translation, Dr. Honeycutt said, is "Shut up!"

Some people seem to have a sixth sense. In addition to hearing, seeing, tasting, smelling, and touching, they also have the ability to be aware, to intuit, while the rest of us wonder what's going on. I think the possibility exists that these people best use their first five senses. They hear before we hear. They see before we see. They feel the tiniest breeze before some of us feel the hurricane-strength wind. While I still make no pretense at being particularly intuitive or having any sort of sixth sense, eventually, as I learned to be quiet and enjoy silence, to pay attention to the world I inhabit, I actually began to hear things I had never heard before. I was no longer merely silent; I became actively aware.

In some old western movies, Native Americans depend on stillness for their survival. They literally put their ears to the ground so they can hear what they need to hear, whether a dry branch crunched nearby or pounding hooves in the distance. I once saw a poster that read, "In quiet places, reason abounds." There are two helpful ways to work on being more attentive to the world in which we live: being silent and observing intentionally.

## Being Silent

Words are not needed for the moon to cross the sky. No sound is required for a smile or a handshake. Nothing is quieter or more beautiful than the angelic face of a baby asleep. A trout slipping through a deep, cold mountain stream gives no hint of a whisper or murmur. A rosebud opening may deserve a fanfare, but none is necessary. If God can be silent on occasion, why can't we? Granted, God can make plenty of noise. Consider thunderstorms and volcanoes. Birds sing, crickets chirp, and tigers roar. But silence is always an option.

Usually, the aggravating noises of our lives are little more than inconveniences and annoyances. Occasionally, however, they rise to the level of being illegal and immoral. We call that "disturbing the peace." But you don't have to elevate the volume of a boom box to disturb the peace. Anything that disrupts tranquility and serenity is a culprit. Cultural clutter surrounds and confounds us. Our civilization, from our television sets to our cell phones to our billboards to our overblown holiday celebrations, interrupts not only our own peace but also the peace of our neighbors . . . and maybe even the peace of God, what the Hebrews call *shalom*. We are over-stimulated by too many visual baubles, too much racket, a cacophony of sights and sounds that mauls and mangles any inner or outer harmony we might have enjoyed. We drink coffee to get revved up, and then we consume alcohol in order to dull our senses. Advertisers compete to get our attention. We need time and space apart from the constant badgering. When is the last time we truly smelled a new scent or savored a new taste?

For me, silence has also involved the reduction of gratuitous movement. Not only do I attempt to be quieter; I also try to be *still*! Anne Morrow Lindberg captures our culture's attitude toward solitary stillness in *Gift from the Sea*:

> If one sets aside time for a business appointment, a trip to the hairdresser, a social engagement, or a shopping expedition, that time is accepted as inviolable. But if one says: I cannot come because that is my hour to be alone, one is considered rude, egotistical or strange. What a commentary on our civilization, when being alone is considered suspect; when one has to apologize for it, make excuses, hide the fact that one practices it—like a secret vice!

Dozens of detractors keep us from enjoying the peace of the moment. What keeps you from enjoying the abundant natural sounds, smells, tastes, sights, and textures that surround you? Likely, you have too many tasks to finish or too many destinations to reach, and you have a schedule to keep. Then, to complicate your life, you encounter an interruption. The phone rings. Rather than responding to the chaos in some new way, you allow yourself to be swept along by the tide. Your attention is averted by ever-increasing numbers of stimuli—magazines, the Internet, trips to Walmart and McDonald's.

In the last few years, I have undertaken several exercises to help me sift through the noise and learn to pay attention better. On a couple of occasions, I have sat quietly and made a list of every sound I heard, every object I saw, or every texture I felt. Once I did this in an automobile dealership in Augusta, Georgia, waiting for the repair of a flat tire. I discovered layers of sound: intrusive noises such as horns honking, radios blaring, metal clanging; secondary noises such as overheard conversation or traffic on the nearby highway; and hidden noises such as the hum of the air-conditioning unit that literally vibrated the building. I suppose that in the right environment, I would even hear the thump of my heartbeat.

On another occasion, I sat in a cemetery in the middle of Brussels, Belgium, and listed forty different sounds I heard, everything from church bells to lawn mowers, from the wind whistling to water trickling, from the cackle of crows to human conversation, from hurrying footsteps to crying babies. What a delightful world we live in, if only we will be still and quiet long enough to notice.

I have discovered that silence nurtures me. Silence promotes healing. One of our local hospitals displays posters in the hall in which a nun holds a finger in front of her mouth in the traditional sign of "Shhh!"

> "When you listen, the benefit is two-fold: You receive necessary information, and you make the other person feel important."
>
> —MARY KAY ASH

Many of the problems of our world are created by people who simply don't know when to hush. I refer primarily to obvious oral blunders that hardly need commentary: gossiping, betraying a confidence, being sarcastic, losing our tempers, being obnoxiously and unnecessarily loud, making promises we cannot keep, ridiculing, slandering, lying, cursing, complaining, and whining. But there are a host of subtle verbal gaffes that also disturb the peace:

• Impatience. "If everybody in Georgia learned tomorrow to keep their mouth shut when they think they've got something that can't wait, there wouldn't be work for maybe eleven lawyers in the state." (Harry Seagraves to Carl Bonner in *Paris Trout*)

• Interruptions. "Quit talking while I'm interrupting."

• Boredom. I have heard there is a rule among certain African tribes that the person speaking in a solemn assembly must stand on one foot while speaking. When he tires of standing on one foot, it is time for him to quit speaking.

• Irrelevance. "Blessed are they who have nothing to say and cannot be persuaded to say it." (James Russell Lowell)

• Stridency. There is an old truism about preachers and politicians: the weaker the point, the louder the volume.

• Lack of context. Telling a joke when seriousness is required: "Like music in mourning is a tale told at the wrong time." (Sirach 22:6)

• The need to have the last word. "Is there never an end of airy words? What a plague your need to have the last word is." (Job 16:3)

• Thoughtless responses. "Your old maxims are proverbs of ash, your retorts, retorts of clay. Silence!" This is a reaction of Job to his unhelpful friends who have been bombarding him with their clichés, their awful attempts to explain his distress.

I once went on a study and planning retreat and committed myself to an extended period of silence. I traveled to Garden City Beach, South Carolina, alone for three days. I determined that I would not speak one word for one full day. After I went to bed one night, I did not speak to anyone the next day, and I finally broke my fast of words on the second morning. I had gone about thirty-six hours without speaking. It was an enlightening experience. First, it was good to discover that I actually had the discipline to follow through on such a commitment. Second, I unintentionally learned something about the world of the deaf. I usually eat in restaurants when I am at the beach, and this occasion was no different. I went to the doughnut shop in the morning and gave the lady behind the counter a note with my order: "2 glazed donuts and 1 medium coffee." She needed clarification about something, so she asked her coworker. I stood directly in front of the clerk. To them, I apparently could not speak, but why did they think I was deaf? I smiled and nodded my head in response to her question, and I was served promptly. I repeated the process at other restaurants (with similar responses) for lunch and dinner, and I loved the experience. I can stay quiet for thirty-six hours! Anytime you discipline yourself to move beyond your comfort zone, you discover things about yourself and your world that you never noticed before.

## Observing Intentionally

The other benefit of being quieter and reducing the chaos of ordinary living is that we begin to experience previously unknown sensations when sights, sounds, tastes, smells, and other information actually pass through the various filters that usually impede them.

I have been called to jury duty several times. Our justice system requires that jurors be exposed to all the facts that are deemed pertinent by the lawyers for the accuser and the defendant. Jury duty is almost always an emotional and mental roller coaster. You hear one set of convincing "facts" as the trial begins. Since they come from a lawyer making an accusation against an individual who seems guilty, you make an initial judgment that he or she has indeed done something wrong—in spite of the judge's instructions that you not make a decision until you hear all the evidence. Then the defendant's lawyer presents an alternate set of "facts." Everything changes! You decide that perpetrator you were on the verge of convicting must have been in the wrong place at the wrong time. Now you see the situation from a different angle. Back and forth the trial goes, first convincing you of one thing, then of another. You have an opportunity, forced upon you by the longevity of the process, to sort out the substance from the clutter. You are not allowed to render a verdict until all involved parties have their say. You are forced to sit silently and listen. Some people are so unaccustomed to sitting quietly that they immediately go to sleep.

Paying attention to the witnesses on both sides of the argument does not turn you into a perfectly objective person. You will inevitably have intuitive reactions about who is trustworthy and who isn't. Indeed, part of the jury process involves determining who is telling the truth by paying attention to body language—by hearing what is said as well as what is not said. Withholding judgment until you hear as much data as possible makes you more accurate in your analysis than if you stopped listening or never listened. People who are unaccustomed to being sensitive observers are forced to remain quiet during this process, even if they don't listen.

You are not allowed to make a final decision until the entire trial is completed and the circumstances and characters involved have been presented to the satisfaction of the judge and both sets of lawyers. Even then, you are required to listen to the input of the other jurors, who may have heard details somewhat differently than you heard them. Listening lets you get past your first reaction, which is often wrong. Sometimes your second and third responses are also incorrect.

As much as possible, we need to apply this type of attention to our entire lives. If we ignore available information, then we will likely make a poor decision. Listening to half of what is said robs us of complete information. Listening only to the gossip side of the news is not likely to help us understand all the facts. Hoping we do not smell smoke, because smoke would force us to get out of a comfortable bed, does not keep the smoke from existing. Not hearing the complaints of our customers does not mean they are not complaining. Failing to see a stop sign does not mean the stop sign is not there. Recently, I heard someone say that one trait of successful individuals is that they are willing and able to name the elephant in the room. While everyone else pretends a problem does not exist, the winning coaches, the thriving executives, the competent doctors, and the helpful teachers boldly name the problem and figure out a way to resolve it.

Being still and paying attention provide the opportunity for clarity and insight. Just as the landscape speeds by in a blur to people in an automobile or a train, so life speeds by those who never slow down to see, to smell, to taste, to touch, or to listen. Several years ago, I attended a continuing education event titled "The Changing Gender Landscape in the Workplace: Empowering Women." The group leader was a woman, as were fifteen of the eighteen participants. As a male, I was there to learn about the issues to which I needed to pay more attention. Our church had a new female associate pastor, and I was in this workshop to learn. I needed to listen. The teacher made introductory comments for about fifteen minutes, then opened the floor for conversation and questions. The other two men in the room made three of the first four remarks. Apparently, in that room, there was no changing gender landscape for them. The women were going to demur, and the men were going to dominate! Since the purpose of the workshop was to help us think about the empowerment of women, I was offended by the aggressiveness of my two male colleagues.

> "A noise is any sound that you do not want or that comes between you and something to which you have chosen to listen."
>
> —WAYNE OATES

Becoming alert to and aware of the nuances of human interaction is essential. Proverbs 10:19 says, "The wise measure their words." Quantifying may not be as dumb as it sounds. If we all "do what comes naturally," then nothing in the workplace will change, even when it needs to change. If we "do what comes naturally," we can grow insensitive to the needs and nuances of life around us.

As I have become more attentive to my world, I have learned to count! Of course, I have known how to add numbers since kindergarten, but now that I am grown, it is time to know what those calculations signify. Social scientists count. Rather than ignoring trends, they actually tally the numbers. They compile statistics. They do not trust their intuition or yours. Do boys get a second or third chance in fifth grade classrooms more often than girls? Educators and sociologists sit in the back of a classroom and count in order to answer that question.

When they want to, ordinary people do their own arithmetic as well. When a grandmother sees four pictures of the other set of grandparents on the mantelpiece and only one picture of her and the grandchild, she takes notice. We pay attention when we are the offended party. We also need to pay attention when we could be the *offending* party.

If you are an employer, group leader, or teacher, consider the following exercise to teach people how to listen. Divide a group of eight to twenty people into two sections, an inner circle and an outer circle. Do not tell them this is an exercise about listening. *Give each group their objective in private so that neither knows the task of the other.* Assign the inner circle an interesting responsibility that relates to your particular group, and encourage them to discuss how to resolve the problem or complete the task. Have the outer circle disperse themselves so they can see and hear the inner circle's conversation and witness the process of decision-making. The outside observers must be totally silent and unobtrusive. As the inner circle goes about its task, certain patterns of behavior will become apparent. Take note.

Give the experience fifteen to twenty minutes, and then have the people in the outer circle relate what they witnessed. Ask questions like those listed below to encourage discussion.

- Did anyone want clearer guidelines and keep turning to the large group leader for clarification?
- Did someone in the inner circle try to become the leader? Did that person succeed? Did a different leader emerge, and if so, how did that happen? Was there competition for the leader's role?
- Did anyone not participate?
- Who made positive contributions and who did not?
- Who kept telling jokes?
- Who was uncomfortable with the process? What was the source of their discomfort? What were the clues to their anxiety? What was their body language?
- Did anyone get angry?
- Did anyone try to make everyone happy and keep the peace?
- Did anyone seem particularly fragile or confused or unsure of himself or herself?

- Was anyone negative throughout the process?
- Did anyone try to engage members of the outer circle in the conversation?
- Were there any in the outer group who, in spite of the instruction for them to be silent, could not resist the temptation to be involved in the conversation?
- Who didn't take the assignment seriously?
- Who took it too seriously?

It is almost impossible to pay attention to such human interaction without becoming more cognizant of one's own foibles. It is likely that those in the outer circle will suspect, even without engaging in the exercise, that they too behave in certain ways. They know if they would have been the joker or the control freak.

The goal is for our eyes and ears to remain open! Once we get the hang of observing intentionally, these skills become second nature. When I'm part of a group these days, I'm usually aware of who says what, and I note the value of their comments. Are they wasting the group's time? Am I wasting the group's time? My late friend Cecil Sherman once commented about a long meeting, "Everything had been said, but not everybody had said it."

Years ago, I read John Molloy's *Dress for Success* (New York: P. H. Wyden, 1975). He recommended an exercise similar to the one I describe above, and I followed his advice. At a meeting of my peers and colleagues, I surreptitiously took notes about what

> "If I speak with the tongues of great orators or angels, but have not love, I am a noisy gong or a clanging cymbal."
> —St. Paul, 1 Corinthians 13:1

each person wore (suit, sport coat, khakis, blue jeans, etc.). Then, based on Molloy's advice, I determined the fashion "mean" and decided that dressing in that particular manner was "safe" in my profession. Three-piece suits may be too much, and shorts and a tee shirt may be too little, but when a male pastor puts on gray slacks and a button-down shirt and a navy blue sport coat, he is usually considered appropriately dressed. Some people may "get it right" intuitively, but the fact that the book existed and was a bestseller for a long time tells me that many people like me needed help. As I have gained skills in observation and assessment, I function better in the real world.

On another occasion, in an attempt to pay better attention to the world, I drove around a five-mile radius of my home and discovered diverse populations about which I knew nothing. I found a body-piercing shop frequented by the "glam metal" crowd. I didn't even know Columbia, South Carolina, had a glam metal crowd! I'm still not sure what a glam metal crowd is, but Columbia has one! I found a Mexican grocery store that had two cow heads in the refrigerated section available for immediate purchase. Sally and I have never needed to go to the grocery store for a cow head. I found a video store for Koreans.

I love this world, and it is bigger and more wonderful than any of us can imagine. It is to our advantage spiritually, economically, and emotionally to be more aware of it and attentive to it than we usually are.

# Chapter 4

# Adolescent Adults

Issue: *Life as a Journey*

---

Objective: I will demonstrate age-appropriate behavior.

---

Most grownups, if they think about it, can point to a few events that were pivotal in their becoming adults—a stern lecture by a boss, the ending of a relationship, a life-threatening accident, a failure or adversity of some sort, discovering where Santa Claus hid his goodies, reading a compelling book. They can divide their lives into chapters: "Before the Event" and "After the Event." Almost always, emotional trauma was involved in the transition!

Every day, someone is in crisis—a marriage disintegrates, a relationship fails, a job ends, health deteriorates. If you are the person in crisis, what do you do? Someone has said, "If you do what you have always done, you will get what you have always gotten!" What does your family script tell you to do? Fight? Run away? Try to talk your way out of your dilemma? Clam up? Offer money? Offer sex? Pout? Certain responses come more naturally than others. Those are probably clues to your life scripts. Maybe those responses usually work. That is probably why you continue to employ them. But do they always work? What if they don't work this time? Do you have only one or two tools or reactions available in your emotional tool kit? In working with people who face an undesirable predicament, the gravest problem I sense is a lack of apparent choices.

In counseling, one of my favorite questions is, "Can you describe your favorite negative feeling?" The person being counseled always knows the answer: disgust or worry or anger or contempt or despair or sarcasm. People intuitively gravitate toward a predictable response—one person spontaneously dominates every situation and another naturally gives in. Those are their scripts.

Immature people fantasize that their circumstances will miraculously improve. They wish somebody or something would hurry up and rescue them. Occasionally, that happens. But the only factor you control in every circumstance is you! You do not need to wait on luck, a hero, or a miracle. Those are fine when they are available, and I like all three, but the one variable that I can always influence is *my* response.

By definition, growth disturbs the status quo: what was is now no more. When my mother learned that I no longer believed in Santa Claus, it

> "You are today where the thoughts of yesterday have brought you, and you will be tomorrow where the thoughts of today take you."
>
> —BLAISE PASCAL

was far more traumatic for her than for me. Sorting out what is real and what is pretend is part of every child's growth. Does the Tooth Fairy really exist? What about Superman? The Easter Bunny? What about God? What about the Lone Ranger and Roy Rogers? Moving from childhood to adolescence is challenging. What is true? What is false? The body with which you were comfortable a year ago begins to betray you. You wonder about the processes of life, which are natural but seem absurd.

Growing up is confusing enough without having to deal with a conspiracy by the grownups of our culture to keep us immature and infantile. My mother had a vested interest in her baby boy staying young. As long as I was a child, she could still claim her own youth. When I asked Mother and Dad the question, "What does 'virgin' mean?" my dad told me to look it up in the dictionary. He wasn't ready for me to have this information, at least not from him. The dictionary was not helpful.

Even outside our family, many older people, even those only slightly senior, preferred to encourage stupidity rather than intelligence. Once we knew what they knew, who would need them? Every kid entering a new phase of life has to undergo certain rites of passage, initiations, many of which are designed to showcase his ignorance and vulnerability. I remember my confusion at my first Pee Wee League baseball practice when one of the older guys yelled that I had picked up a left-handed bat and needed a right-handed bat. I had been playing pick-up baseball for years already, and had never heard of different bats, so the challenge caught me off guard. As I sprinted back to the dugout to grab a different bat, the other kids began to heckle me. I had been the victim of a prank. The kidder and the other kids knew, at least for now, that I was ignorant. What else did they know that I didn't know?

Insiders have always used privileged information, from secret hand-shakes to an Ivy League education, to keep their clubs elite and exclusive and to keep the masses at bay. Our culture, especially the wealthy and powerful in our communities, have also benefited from having the rest of us be as compliant and unquestioning as possible: "Do what you are told"; "Don't make waves"; "Don't ask questions"; "We're doing this for your own good"; "Play by the rules." But even the dullest, most ignorant, most obsequious kids must become adults, at least in some ways. After all, it is socially unac-ceptable to continue writing letters to Santa Claus after you are married. Teachers scold high school students who continue to behave like elementary school children.

The challenge is to grow up all the way—mentally, physically, academi-cally, socially, emotionally, and spiritually. We would wonder about a young mother who woke up on Easter morning searching for what the Easter Bunny brought her, not knowing she was now supposed to be the Easter Bunny. We would universally acknowledge her naïveté. Yet, we think it is perfectly normal for an entire assembly of young mothers to gather socially for breakfast on Saturday morning, wearing basically the same outfits and talking endlessly about the same topics because they are afraid to be different and fearful of standing out from the group.

Many narcissistic young adults and their families seem to think it is normal for financial support to extend to age thirty and beyond, with the parents working and the grown "children" unemployed. Many of these ado-lescent adults spend their days playing video games with their buddies, eating pizza and drinking beer for dinner every night, and then consuming leftover pizza for breakfast every morning (or afternoon when they finally wake up).

What are the marks of maturity? How do we grow up? Is gaining experi-ence and insight inevitable? Shouldn't all forty-year-olds be less fearful about the opinions of others than their twelve-year-old children? Or do we all grow at a different pace? Do some adolescents or young adults "fail to thrive" emo-tionally just as some babies fail to thrive physically?

For most of us, growth comes when we discover new insights by becom-ing even minimally independent, by paying attention, and by being curious. When I grew suspicious about the reality of Santa, I snooped around the house until I found where my parents hid the presents. When my parents failed to answer my sex education questions, I looked elsewhere for answers . . . and got them! When my culture taught me, by words and actions, that black people were somehow inferior to white people, and my intuition questioned that premise, I began questioning authority. Unfortunately, I accepted what my culture taught me about the second-class status of women until I was an adult!

Of course, everything my parents and my culture taught me was not wrong. That was and is the dilemma. How do we sort it out? What combination of characteristics is required to move me from the ignorance of youth into a happy and productive adulthood?

I would always rather learn new information in a pain-free manner. Why wait until I have a wreck while driving drunk before I learn that driving drunk has grave consequences? Why wait until I get AIDS from unprotected sex before I learn that unprotected sex is a dangerous practice?

A life-altering event happened to me in college. I was a member of the Student Senate at Clemson University, and usually we debated such banal questions as whether or not the male senators should wear a coat and tie to the meetings. Occasionally, to the chagrin of the deans, we actually dealt with something of substance. In the late 1960s, overt racism was a larger fact of life on our conservative campus than were drugs. In the Deep South, the Civil War, more than 100 years in our past, still stirred far more emotion than World War II. The Second World War was history. The Civil War seemed like a current event. The Confederate Battle Flag was prominently and vigorously waved at our football and basketball games.

> "The dogmas of the quiet past are inadequate to the stormy present. The occasion is piled high with difficulty, and we must rise with the occasion. As our case is new, so we must think anew and act anew."
>
> —ABRAHAM LINCOLN

Someone put forth a motion in our Student Senate that flaunting the Confederate flag should not be allowed in our sports arenas. Ours was a newly integrated campus. I was against the motion. I was proud of my Dixie heritage. I did not think of myself as a racist; I loved the Deep South. I loved our songs, our heroes, our food (grits, fatback, collards, barbeque, turnips, okra and cornbread), and the Rebel Yell (mine was louder than anybody's). My accent, then and now, is deep-fried and smothered in red-eye gravy. I was and am about as Southern as a human can be! But I was in college getting a "liberal arts" education, and for the first time in my life, I was aware of a larger world. I had never been in school with a person of African heritage until I got to college. In my culture, we still used the "N" word casually.

A pretty Jewish woman sat beside me during the debate on the motion to ban the Confederate flag in the football stadium. She whispered to me, "Waving the Confederate flag in the face of a black person seems to me to be no different than waving a Nazi flag in my face."

I had never thought about that! She was right. Period. I learned something that day. I voted for the resolution. I am pleased to say that Confederate flags are no longer waved at Clemson University on game day in the stadium. Something shifted in me that day. I changed an old way of thinking. I grew up a bit.

Growth is not automatic. Everyone does not mature emotionally or morally in the same way and at the same pace, any more than they do physically. Gaining age-appropriate attitudes and behavior seems like a sensible goal to me. Fifty-year-old adults should not act as self-consumed and unaware as children. Imagine sitting in a church for a funeral, and the two acolytes, ten-year-old boys sitting on the front row during the eulogy, are talking and jabbing each other with the candle-lighters as if they were swords. One seems utterly unaware of his environment. The other seems nervous but doesn't know how to disengage himself without his friend calling him a sissy. This is exactly how some adults appear to those who have to endure their foolish behavior. Why won't those adolescent adults grow up? Why are they stuck? Why has their emotional growth been stunted? We know the other guy started it. But they are adults, and they have choices.

## Middle School Immaturity: Sally's List

In 1 Corinthians 13:11, Paul writes, "When I was a child, I spoke like a child, thought and reasoned like a child. But, when I grew up, I put away childish habits." My wife Sally is a middle school teacher. She and I have been working on the same problem our entire adult lives, but with different population subsets. I have mentored, taught, counseled, and coached adults, challenging them to grow up, to get unstuck from the old habits they have repeated for a lifetime. Sometimes those habits are merely unproductive and

benign. Other times, they are posi-
tively malignant and destructive.
Sally has worked for four decades
with twelve- to fourteen-year-old
girls and boys. She teaches math to
seventh and eighth grade adolescents. I asked Sally, my resident
expert, "What are the signs of matu-

> "No person is your friend
> who demands your
> silence, or denies your
> right to grow."
>
> —ALICE WALKER

rity you hope to see in your middle school students?" Or, stated negatively,
"What are the signs of immaturity?" This is Sally's list of the signs of immaturity and examples of them:

1. Insecurity
   - "I was afraid you would take off points if I did that."
   - "I'm ugly and nobody likes me."
   - "I don't want to hold the hamster. It looks like a rat."
   - The child separates himself or herself from all the other children.
   - The child clings to the teacher or a particular friend or group.
2. Failure to Listen
   - "I didn't hear you say we were having a test."
   - "I didn't see anything written on the back of the paper."
   - "I didn't hear the bell ring."
   - The child interrupts when someone else is talking.
3. Irresponsibility
   - "I lost my calculator."
   - "The dog ate my homework."
   - "I didn't know it was time for class to start."
   - "Somebody stole my pencil, and I couldn't find another one."
   - The child plays catch with a baseball during class.
4. Lack of Effort
   - "I didn't have time."
   - "I'm hungry because I forgot to eat breakfast."
   - "I didn't know we were supposed to go to the gym."
   - "Oops. I didn't remember to brush my teeth."
   - "I got a gerbil for Christmas, but Momma takes care of it."
5. Inaccurate, disproportionate, inappropriate, inflexible words and behavior
   - Insert the sound of a child wailing desperately when her knee is
     skinned, the "drama queen syndrome." Every two-year-old does this

reflexively. Twelve-year-olds should do it less, and fifty-year-olds should do it not at all.
- "Tell her to quit looking at me."
- "There have been no good movies all year."
- "Everybody was doing it."
- "You never let me go first."
- Insert a big, obnoxious "BURP" here.

6. Cruelty
- "You're fat and ugly and nobody likes you."
- The child moves his desk away from someone on an assigned team because of contempt for that person's perceived lack of personal hygiene.
- The child hits another person when she is angry.
- "Your cat died? That's funny."
- "You can't be on our team."

Around the age of thirty, I finally recognized myself as a flawed adult, physically mature yet emotionally stunted. I lived in an adult body but was guilty of acting as if I were still a twelve-year-old for whom someone else was ultimately responsible. Some adults enjoy that role, especially if they are able to find a parent, a lover, or someone else who is willing to assume responsibility for their lives. They seek marriages or jobs in which someone else will take care of them. I had no interest in turning responsibility for my life over to anyone else, so I began to make changes in my life.

Soon I wanted this same "maturity" for my family and friends and, for that matter, everyone else. Converts are easy to hate. Once someone finds the secret to losing weight, getting off drugs, staying happily married, or living a full and meaningful life, he or she wants everybody else to have the same experience. I am sure I have irritated a lot of people over the years in trying to convince them that there was a better life on the adult side of age sixteen! No wonder we resist people who want us to change. They irritate us. They want us to grow up and overcome our adolescence, and sometimes we resent that.

I have mostly made peace with the fact that I am not responsible for making everybody act the way I wish they would. I cannot make other individuals responsible or keep them from being irresponsible. Jesus said the poor will always be with us. The irresponsible will always be with us, too. So will the fearful. So will the class clowns and the bullies. However, if we want to grow up, I can think of no better place to start than with Sally's list. Here are ways that adults, from thirty-year-olds to eighty-year-olds, remain childish:

1. Insecurity
   - "I was afraid you would leave."
   - The person avoids eye contact.
   - "I was worried about what the others would think."
   - The person seeks attention with loud and boisterous behavior.
   - "I wasn't sure which to do, so I did neither."
   - "I was afraid I would lose money."
   - The person wonders who is watching and what they will think.
2. Failure to Listen
   - "When did he say that? I never heard him say that."
   - "I don't want to hear her opinion."
   - The person interrupts with an answer before the question is finished.
   - The person is non-empathetic and doesn't seem to take another person's thoughts or ideas seriously.
3. Irresponsibility
   - "Nobody ever taught me about credit cards."
   - The person gossips about others.
   - "I think the government is to blame."
   - "My family is big-boned. That's why I'm large."
   - "If you think I'm bad, you should see my brother."
   - "She was supposed to take care of that."
   - "Somebody should have warned us."
   - "The alarm didn't go off."
   - "I just can't remember to pay the bills on time."
4. Lack of Effort
   - "I've never even been in our town library."
   - "I can't ever find my driver's license."
   - The person sleeps through a job interview (or while at work).
   - "I quit."
   - The person is unwilling to try to talk about a problem.
5. Inaccurate, disproportionate, inappropriate, or inflexible words or behavior
   - Loud clothes. Loud mouth.
   - Big spender even when the credit card is over the limit.

- "He wasn't just *two* minutes late. He was *six* minutes late."
- "I already know how to do this."
- Acting silly on a solemn occasion.
- "Can you believe she wore that shade of lipstick?"
- "You spent more money on her Christmas present than on mine."
- "I'll apologize after he apologizes."
- "You've never supported me in my job."
- "My momma is going to die when she hears that."

6. Cruelty
- "You're still fat and ugly and nobody likes you."
- The person is manipulative and intends to get his own way no matter what.
- The person hits someone else when she is angry.
- "Your children don't want you to visit."
- "Anybody who believes that is stupid."

Of course, many of our mistakes fit under more than one category. For example, having an affair is both irresponsible and hurtful. The flip sides of these negative traits comprise the outline of this book. We function best as mature adults when we

1. have courage.
2. listen and pay attention.
3. are responsible and self-motivated.
4. are empowered.
5. know the facts and use them wisely
6. are kind and gracious.

## The Narrative of Human Growth

Of course, Sally's list is not the first ever devised to describe emotional growth and movement from childhood to adulthood.

Erik Erikson delineated eight stages of human development from birth to death. He felt that people needed to pass through these stages or risk being stuck at some level of immaturity. (See chapter 8 for a fuller explanation of his model and those described below.)

Eric Berne introduced Transactional Analysis to explain why we behave (or misbehave) as we do, distinguishing between responses of parents, children, and mature adults. Why do you act differently than I do in the same circumstances? Did our parents train us, either intentionally or unintentionally, to respond in a certain way? Of course they did! Some of us approach life full of fear that we will make a mistake, while others are unconcerned about the impact of errors. Were your parents critical or nurturing or a combination of both? What did their words teach you? What did you "catch" by watching their behavior?

Murray Bowen and Rabbi Ed Friedman introduced the Family Systems Theory. The core of this model for understanding emotional development (or the lack thereof) concerns how we relate to others in our family system (or work system or community system). Crudely speaking, as long as Big Daddy is out there wielding a club and reminding everyone that he is the alpha male in the social system, he will continue in that role until someone knocks him out with a bigger club and takes his place. Thus, a sixty-year-old heir to the throne still carries the juvenile-sounding title of "Prince" until the patriarch or matriarch dies. Only then is he free to be fully empowered. Until then, no matter how rich or famous, he is a wannabe, not yet completely mature. Sons and daughters fill roles as the Smart Kid, the Dumb Jock, Daddy's Girl, the Little Brother, the Rebel, the Artist, or the Sassy Daughter. They accept the short, one- or two-word assessment of who they are and act accordingly: Flirt, Bum, Stupid, Angelic. As helpful as a "diagnosis" can be, labels can also create problems. If I have Attention Deficit Disorder (ADD), does that keep me from being responsible for my actions for the next thirty years? Sometimes adult children literally fly to the ends of the earth to get away from such "scripts." As long as an all-A student is in the house, the child who makes B's is runner-up, second-place, and may even be considered a loser.

> "Life is a process of becoming, a combination of states we have to go through. Where people fail is that they wish to elect a state and remain in it. This is a kind of death."
>
> —ANAIS NIN

Everybody has a story, and I have yet to find anyone whose narrative is not fascinating. But all of our accounts are incomplete. There are chapters yet to be written. What we do next will determine whether we bore even ourselves.

A device that novelists and television scriptwriters use, called a "story arc," explains the growth and development of a fictional character. It's not much of a drama or a life if the story line is that a person is born, lives, and then dies. The end. Dull. Boring. Tedious. Lifeless. Monotonous. Same old, same old.

Instead, drama and life worth living have many chapters or acts, each of which has its own arc. In an exciting existence, what *was* is not what *is*, and what *is* is not what *will be*. Depending on which source you use, somewhere between five to eight events must happen to produce a meaningful arc. These guidelines help create a strong story.

1. *A status quo exists.* This is who you are, your life situation, the what, when, and where of your existence. Life rolls along—food, television, sex, sleep, sports, hobbies, whatever. Then something happens. Fiction writers need a precipitating or trigger event, a crisis, or an opportunity. It can involve a poisoned apple, a seduction by a sexy woman, or an automobile accident.

2. *A quest is undertaken.* Quests are the stuff of great literature: Quixote or Ulysses. The mission or effort may involve a literal journey, going somewhere, or it may be next door, getting a degree at the local community college. Or the "journey" may be a wimp's attempt to return safely and without adventure to the previous status quo.

3. *While on this quest, when the character does something she has never done before, surprises are bound to arise.* She meets complications and conflicts and reversals of fortune. Aliens, alligators, or other antagonists will likely appear. She encounters enemies on the journey and the quest becomes an ordeal. Life gets complicated. Some people become adversaries—parents, bosses, colleagues, spouses, and children. Disturbances of the status quo happen when someone changes any part of a life equation. People are fearful of what they do not understand.

4. *The hero must make a critical choice.* He has new insight and new options. Does he fight or flee? It is decision time, for good or for ill.

5. *The character's decision results in a climax.* Whatever happens, her life is altered. She could be (at least for a while) gloriously happy for persevering to the peak through the pain. She has reached her mountaintop, an

epiphany, release and relief. Or he may have a new self-understanding as a coward.

Tragedy and comedy occur in great literature because the classics reflect real life. Everyone does not make the right decision on every adventure and at every turn. Romeo and Juliet die, as does Cleopatra. Sometimes, death and life go together. Martin Luther King, Jr., was assassinated, but his mission continued after his death. Character A learns from her mistakes, learns from the aggravations of others, moves forward, and matures. Character B returns to her oblivion. Nothingness. Lifelessness. Emptiness. (The good news is that unless life is truly over, meaning death, the character returns to status quo. Life often gives us second chances. Sometimes, of course, it does not.)

6. *Conflicts are resolved and status changes.* Grief counselors call this the affirmation of life. Transformation does not happen glibly or quickly, but it happens. With a positive resolution, we say the character lived happily ever after. Now it is time to start a new chapter.

# Chapter 5

# Quit Whining!

> Objective: I will accept responsibility for what is actually under my control, or should be under my control, and I will not accept responsibility for what is under someone else's control, or for other life circumstances over which I have no control.

I am continually flabbergasted by people who make one bad decision after another and are then surprised when they experience bad results. What did they think would happen? Bad choices usually result in bad consequences. Many people live as if they hope something will magically clean up their messes. Whom do they think is responsible for their decisions?

Are there occasions when we are not responsible? In a summer school ethics class I took between college and seminary, Professor George Kelsey of Drew University outlined three circumstances in which a person is *not* morally responsible.

1. We are *not* responsible when we do something as a result of a reflex action. If I am on guard duty, responsible for the safety and well-being of a platoon, but I sneeze as the result of a bug flying into my left nostril, and the enemy finds us as a result of hearing my sneeze and somehow manages to kill everyone except for me, then I am not morally responsible for the deaths of my comrades. (That will probably never happen to you.)

2. We are *not* responsible when we do something as the result of an irresistible, overpowering, external impetus. If I shove you, and your momentum causes you to knock down someone else, and they are harmed as a result of being pushed, you are not morally responsible for their injury. (That could happen to you.)

3. When we are ignorant and irreversibly so, that is, we have ignorance we can do nothing about, we are *not* morally responsible. Dr. Kelsey called this "invincible ignorance." Most of us do not have to be as uninformed as we are. Invincible ignorance can provide moral mercy for mentally challenged or mentally ill people, but it does not let lazy people off the hook. Invincible ignorance concedes that children are blameless prior to what some religious traditions call "the age of accountability." A two-year-old is not morally responsible for a temper tantrum. A twenty-year-old is. The theory of invincible ignorance lets doctors off the hook for not prescribing the correct medication for your disease if that medication is still undiscovered in the Amazon jungle somewhere. If, however, that medicine has been discovered, but your doctor does not prescribe it because he or she does not reasonably keep up with the medical journals or attend continuing education conferences, then your doctor could be morally responsible.

> "We are responsible for our own behavior, but we are not responsible for other people's reactions; nor are they responsible for ours. . . . We put our energy into taking responsibility for other people's feelings, thoughts and behavior and hand over to others responsibility for our own."
>
> —HARRIET G. LERNER, *THE DANCE OF ANGER*

If you don't make good decisions because you never bothered to think about certain problems you will inevitably face, or you failed to ask people who could help you, or you failed to seek counsel from relevant books or even the Internet, then you are morally responsible for your poor choices.

The process of physical, emotional and intellectual maturation changes the acceptability of your ignorance annually. We don't expect a middle-aged person to be as clueless as a teenager about certain issues. While there are exceptions, adolescents are rarely required to think about the death of a parent. They are working out other life issues. Death isn't high on their list. Sex is. But a fifty-year-old woman with an eighty-year-old mother who has never thought about the possibility of death is morally and emotionally immature and irresponsible.

Scott Peck began his classic, *The Road Less Traveled*, with the much-quoted sentence, "Life is difficult." We may wish it weren't so, but postponing or dodging our responsibility does not make troubles go away. It simply means we have abdicated control or responsibility for them to someone else. Individuals often shirk responsibility for their own actions and inactions. Many even prefer to whine about the unfairness of life!

Negative life circumstances that are the result of another person's misbehavior or malfeasance are one kind of problem. However, even if another person is at fault for putting you in a difficult situation, there is always some possibility that you can redeem the circumstances. Alcoholics Anonymous and Gamblers Anonymous meetings, churches, synagogues, and temples are full of women and men who have overcome childhood trauma, abuse, and other tragedies. Most other people may not have experienced your particular horror story, but somewhere on this planet is someone who was poorer, sicker, and/or more mistreated than you were who has overcome obstacles to achieve some form of success. Criminals have gone straight. Prostitutes have turned off their red light. Alcoholics have sobered up. The temperamental person has found peace. The obese have lost weight. Someone who has been married and divorced five times already finally figures out how to stay in an intimate relationship. The loner makes friends. The obsessive-compulsive relaxes.

I heard of a fascinating process used during World War II for officer selection in the United States military. A group of soldiers was given a task to do by cooperating with each other and competing against other teams working on the same task. The participants did not know that a saboteur was included in each cluster to compromise the group's effectiveness. Obstructions were deliberately created to slow the pace. Obnoxious suggestions were made. When the smoke cleared and the process ended, the teams discovered that the real competition had nothing to do with speed, as compared to the other teams, but with how they coped with frustration. Even though they were not responsible for the aggravation caused by their noncompliant teammate, they were accountable for how they responded to the mess he created.

As I have looked in my own mirror, I can name three common themes that are routinely involved when I am tempted to shirk responsibility. They are defensiveness, denial, and blame.

## Defensiveness

One day I heard myself grousing to a friend that I had been "fussed at" by someone earlier that day. Those were defensive words. I was protecting myself against a supposed aggressor, making my antagonist a bad guy for chastising sweet, innocent, innocuous me. I was looking for sympathy. I felt I had been victimized by an antagonist. I went home that evening and studied a dictionary and a thesaurus so that I would at least tell myself the truth about what had transpired. I made two lists to describe the act of being questioned by someone verbally:

| Strong Words | Mild Words |
|---|---|
| accosted | agreed to disagree |
| accused | commented on |
| attacked | conferred |
| blamed | consulted |
| castigated | critiqued |
| censured | dealt with |
| challenged | differed |
| chastised | disapproved |
| chided | discussed |
| condemned | evaluated |
| criticized | mentioned |
| denounced | noticed |
| destroyed | quibbled |
| fussed at | reviewed |
| humiliated | talked over |
| judged | talked with me about |
| put down | took exception to |
| scolded | |
| upbraided | |

In retrospect, honesty compels me to acknowledge that my critic had merely commented on something I said. But my defenses were so high that I perceived any disagreement as a personal attack. An acquaintance recently told me his boss "went ballistic," when, after some analysis, a milder description would have been more accurate. Had his supervisor really set into motion some sort of "nuclear option" that would be unimaginably destructive, or had his boss merely given him a verbal reprimand to be more careful next time? My observation was that my acquaintance, not his boss, had over-reacted.

As a person who hates confrontation, my unease is not limited to after-the-fact reactions. Sometimes I employ my defenses even before they are needed. In a business setting several years ago, I proposed to my board that we investigate the possibility of a rather large undertaking. I must have rambled on with ten minutes of preliminary justifications and rationalizations before someone interrupted me and said, "Marion, all you are asking us to do right now is form a committee, right? Is that all?" When I answered in the affirmative, he made a motion that we form a committee and let the board meeting move forward. That is what happened.

Defensiveness, I have learned, is motivated by anxiously viewing the world as if everyone is a critical parent. The root of this emotion is the fear of failure; we're afraid we won't make everybody happy. When someone is displeased about something, defensive people feel judged and accused. This is the result of low self-esteem.

Years ago, following a conversation with my mother, with whom I was often defensive, I had an "Aha!" moment. She disputed a comment I made by saying, "I thought you told me . . . ." When I unraveled the matter later, it turns out that the two accounts being compared were basically in agreement in 99 out of 100 details. Mother, as mothers will, had zeroed in on the one discrepancy and took our conversation there. When such a pattern has existed from childhood onward, it's no wonder defensiveness exists! You are not allowed error in any particular. Perfection is required, but since no one is perfect, you have to figure out a way to justify what you did and why you did it.

Do you sometimes think of the perfect response an hour later or the next day? As I have become less defensive, I have more often found myself responding appropriately and acting reasonably right in the middle of the situation instead of later. These days I am more likely to ask a pertinent question that moves us forward rather than getting stuck in my own self-justifications.

In *Getting the Love You Want* (New York: H. Holt and Co., 2008), Harville Hendrix has this insight: "In most interactions with your spouse, you are actually safer when you lower your defenses than when you keep them engaged, because your partner becomes your ally, not an enemy." I like the idea of turning people I perceive as my enemies into my allies.

Furthermore, when a person attacks someone else, he or she is usually afraid of something. For some reason, the attacked individual represents that terror. If you can respond to the attacker's fear rather than to the attack, you will both be better off. We need to change the question from "Why are they picking on me?" to "What are they afraid of?" or even "Why are they afraid of me?" Someone's anger, thus anxiety, actually means the other person, the one being attacked, has more power in a given situation. Why be defensive?

## Denial

The JoHari window, developed in 1955 by Joseph Luft (Jo) and Harry Ingram (Hari), is a helpful tool for understanding that parts of our lives are hidden from even the most astute and self-aware among us.

| 1<br><br>+<br><br>+<br><br>(Arena) | 2<br><br>+<br><br>-<br><br>(Blind Spot) |
|---|---|
| 3<br><br>-<br><br>+<br><br>(Hidden/Facade) | 4<br><br>-<br><br>-<br><br>(Unknown) |

For the purposes of this illustration, every person's life is a window made of four panes or quadrants.

1. The top left quadrant (1) is called the *Arena* because everybody can watch what happens in it. The Arena has two plus marks, indicating that anybody can see directly and clearly into that window pane, that quadrant, at any time. The Arena is public knowledge about you or me, what "anybody" knows: name, age (more or less), skin color, height, how big your nose is, your job, where you live, how many pets you have. These facts are known or can easily be known to you (+) and to others (+).

2. Quadrant 2, in the upper right, has one plus sign and one minus sign to signify that there are some things other people know about you (+) that you don't know about yourself (-). This is your *Blind Spot*. You may have bad breath and not know it. At a deeper lever, your friends may know you are depressed. Maybe you bring gloom into any room you enter, and your friends are concerned about you, but you have no idea they see you that way. Your boss may know you will be promoted on Monday, and you aren't aware of it. Your family may know your drinking is out of control, while you think you drink like everybody else, just to be sociable. People on the board to which you were recently elected may think you are the biggest mistake they ever made and wish they could get rid of you. Alternatively, most people may see you as the glue that holds your office together. You are why they feel good about coming to work in the morning, but no one has ever told you that. The Blind Spot can be positive or negative.

3. The third quadrant is what is known to you (+) and not to others (-), unless you choose for them to know it: Social Security number, when you and your significant other last had sex, or if you have ever had sex, whether or not you sleep with a teddy bear, your salary, what pills you take before you go to bed at night. These are hidden from other people unless you choose to let them know more about your personal life than they can know just by looking. This is the *Hidden Quadrant*, the façade or face you put forward to the public. One of the reasons many people fear counseling is their belief that a counselor/therapist will be able to see right through them, that they will be "found out." They have no desire to reveal what they have worked hard to keep hidden.

4. Quadrant 4, the *Unknown*, has two minuses (-) (-) that indicate things about you that no one knows, yourself included. You may have a brain tumor growing inside you right now, affecting the way you think or act. I had an acquaintance during graduate school who began acting out of character. He was dead six months later from a brain tumor. Or you and everyone else may be unaware that the person who just moved in next door will become the best friend you have ever had.

Plenty of reality exists in every windowpane. All four panes or quadrants are necessary for giving an authentic and comprehensive picture of every human being.

The hidden stuff usually causes the nastiest problems. If you know something other people need to know and you don't tell them, your *hidden agenda* can create enormous pain and ill health. Hidden agendas generally waste time and energy. Several years ago, I was on a committee assigned to plan a charitable event. Six of us met for an hour, with useful, energetic input from five of the participants. After fifty-five minutes, one woman stood up in tears and told us she wanted the event to be just as it had been the year before. She wanted a memorial to her friend who had planned the event the year before and had since died. That was okay with the rest of us. We could have saved six hours of hard work if she had told us her agenda in the first five minutes. She had a silent proposal or agenda that no one else was privy to. That was irritating and wasteful of our time and energy.

If you have information that is important for solving a problem to create a positive outcome, put it on the table. Don't hide it. That is your responsibility. If you want your husband to give you flowers for Valentine's, or if you want your girlfriend not to give you a surprise birthday party, say so to the individual who needs to know! Mind reading does not work.

Far more important than the smaller agendas that waste a bit of time or are minor annoyances are the "dirty big secrets" of our lives, things like bulimia, visits to prostitutes, criminal behavior, child battering, massive credit card debt, or prescription drug addiction. I believe that every emotional or spiritual problem anyone has ever faced has been conquered by somebody. I don't suggest that success will be easy, but I do believe human lives can change, can be transformed. Sometimes the victories are measured in inches. Sometimes they are measured in miles. Success begins when you admit there is a problem. Then make progress where

> "Finish each day and be done with it. . . . You have done what you could; some blunders and absurdities no doubt crept in; forget them as soon as you can. Tomorrow is a new day; you shall begin it well and serenely."
>
> —Ralph Waldo Emerson

you can. Stop the little stuff that feeds the big stuff. Pay attention. Get to know yourself better.

That returns us to quadrant 2, regarding what people know about you that they haven't told you. If you want to know something, it is your responsibility to ask and to listen. This is where children, parents, spouses, best friends, and sometimes even strangers are helpful. Even when you aren't sure you want to hear the truth, somebody will tell you if you are willing to listen.

One of our sorrier human reactions is to "kill the messenger." We don't want to hear what someone is telling us, so we accuse the messenger (the relative, the counselor, the newspaper editor, the prophet) for causing the problem.

"He's too negative," someone says.

"She always takes your side," he laments.

"Stop my subscription immediately," we write.

"You're fired," the trustees say.

Too many people prefer to function like ostriches, with their heads in the ground and rears in the air, ignoring the obvious and displaying the ludicrous. One of the reasons kings kept court jesters around was to give somebody permission to point out publicly, or maybe privately, with a light and humorous touch, what everyone else was already saying secretively outside the king's earshot. Lunatics, clowns, and children could often articulate, and get away with it, what everyone else was thinking but afraid to utter: "The emperor is naked." Even if they make us uncomfortable and occasionally angry, we need people who will tell us the truth rather than just bow to us and say, "Yes, Your Honor"; "Whatever you say, Your Holiness"; "Sure, Dad"; "Anything you desire, Mom"; "Of course, you are right, Boss. You are always right." Frederick Buechner wrote in *The Magnificent Defeat*, "In the realm of our blindness, we need poets or children or lunatics to show us the miracles we do not notice" (New York: HarperOne, 1985).

Ultimately, *you* have responsibility for all four of *your* quadrants. Why should anybody else be responsible for you? If you are comatose, you have no choice, but if you are functional enough to read, you can understand yourself better than anyone else can, and you can help yourself live an improved life. If you need an objective person, and I believe we all do, secure a life coach, a mentor, a therapist, a pastor, a rabbi, a guru, a guide, a tutor, a mentor, a counselor, someone, anyone, who will be honest enough to help you see yourself as others see you. A counselor can give you feedback on reality, or at least an alternate perception of reality. Myron Madden, in *The Power to Bless*, wrote, "A person seldom has the ability or the courage to see himself by himself" (Nashville: Broadman, 1970). The panes in the windows of our lives are tinted in ways that obscure perfect vision. Instead, they tend to become cloudy, foggy, misty, and dirty. We almost certainly need someone else to help us see through the grime.

Having objective advisers is crucial. Having supportive family and friends is nice, but we do not grow when someone merely affirms and comforts us. Being valued, warts and all, is important. I will never forget the advice of my friend Larry Abernathy when I was in the midst of a crisis: "Surround yourself with people who care for you."

Growth, on the other hand, requires challenges, new insight, and new actions. I have observed a situation recently in which a colleague has been self-destructing, largely because of bad counsel from his family and closest friends. The presenting issue becomes almost irrelevant. The question for each of us is, "How will I use this crummy situation to grow?" Being rescued by our family and friends and being encouraged by our closest advisers to engage in unhealthy follow-up behaviors (such as blaming) with no sense of shared culpability is unproductive. There is always something I can learn. This is a fine and difficult line to walk. You did not cause your spouse to become an alcoholic or your boss to become abusive. But wouldn't you want to know if you engaged in enabling behavior? Don't you want your next marriage to be better? Don't you want to know how to function differently the next time you encounter a bully for a boss? Yes, the situation is awful. Now where do you go from here? What can you learn? How can you respond differently? There are many ways to react to every life circumstance, even the horrid ones.

I can ask a simple question, "How much longer will it take you?" and ten different people hear ten different questions. One hears hostility and anger left over from a disapproving parent ("You are always late and irresponsible. How much longer will you be? Hurry up!"), and another hears a straightforward question about time and answers, "I have about an hour left on this project."

The more we can know about ourselves, the more options we have for appropriate response. If I am unaware of my own tendencies, then I will almost always do what comes naturally, and act out of long-held scripts. That is not necessarily a satisfactory reaction. What seems acceptable to us, our life scripts, our habits, our intuitions, may be adequate some of the time and deadly on other occasions.

Codependent behavior illustrates how natural responses can cause harm. Codependents are those who instinctively help addicted persons maintain their addictions. Therefore, two people are hooked. Many spouses of alcoholics have decided, subconsciously, that they like their spouse better drunk. "At least he was predictable then. Now that he is sobering up, I don't know what will happen next." Life is no longer stable in their family. It doesn't have to be this way. In this example, if you are related to someone who is addicted, then AlAnon, a sister organization to Alcoholics Anonymous, can help you see yourself through the eyes of other people who have experienced life in some of the same ways as you. One of the first things AA teaches is to "Take a searching moral inventory" of yourself. There is nothing easy about this, but it will change your life for the better.

Quadrant 4 is not unknowable. It is merely unknown. The goal is not to eliminate quadrants 2 through 4, but to have them no larger than they need to be. Some matters are private.

Self-understanding is a lifelong process. As you get to know yourself better and become clearer about the world you live in and the people who surround you, you will become the mature person you desire to be.

## Blame

Blame is an unkind form of irresponsibility. Criticizing others for what happens in my life means not only that I resist self-responsibility, but that I go one step farther. Blame makes someone or something else responsible for what happens in my life: my parents, the government, my spouse, my employer, my bad back, my skin color, or my acne. If you want to change a habit or script or circumstance, one of the problems with blaming is that someone else has way too much jurisdiction over your life.

Books have been written about the "victimization of America." We want to hold somebody else culpable for every adverse event. A bumper sticker reminds us that sometimes ugly, smelly, gross, inconvenient, putrid stuff just happens. There is no way to avoid some events.

You always always have options about how to respond. *You* choose. If you believe that you don't, think about this: Dad wakes his children at 7 a.m. on Saturday morning, and predictably they moan and groan.

> "The problem of distinguishing what we are and what we are not responsible for in this life is one of the greatest problems of human existence. It is never completely solved."
>
> —SCOTT PECK, *THE ROAD LESS TRAVELED*

"Leave us alone!" Then Dad says, "Get dressed. I have a surprise. We are going to Disney World today." Do you think there will be a change in the attitude of those children? Of course. It is still Saturday morning, and their sleep has still been interrupted. Those facts haven't changed. The change came in their attitude. We all have a choice in how we face each day and each decision. Every day is not a Disney day, but maybe more would be if our attitudes were different.

One component of good mental health is the awareness that there are some circumstances when no one is in charge. That sentence will infuriate some people. They think someone must be accountable. These are people who simply cannot accept the reality that there is not enough money in the world, not enough time in the world, not enough of anything in the world to control every event. After the December 26, 2004, tsunami, I heard people attempting to assign blame. Can some person you know control earthquakes on the bottom of the ocean?

In the story of Snow White, the wicked stepmother blames the mirror when it tells her Snow White is fairer than she is. Beauty is not a mirror's responsibility! That is the kind of behavior we might wish were limited to fairy tales. Unfortunately, every day, people act just as foolishly. Those who scream the loudest and blame the most are those with least control of their own lives. Someone once told me, "I must do something" is always a better option and will solve more problems than "Something must be done."

# Chapter 6

# Who Are You?

Issue: Identity

Objective: I will acknowledge my complexity.

We are complicated. A long paragraph, even a book, is not enough to explain each individual. Yet we try to describe people with the fewest words possible: trophy wife, AIDS patient, geek, jock, flirt, fool. But one word or two or even ten won't do. Even the obvious attributes of my physical description would require a couple of pages: height, weight, age, gender, scars, birthmarks. In the face alone, consider nose size, ear size, number of teeth, brightness and health of teeth, eye color, hair color, skin color, freckles, and wrinkles.

Some of these seem unalterable, nonnegotiable. Yet people wear high-heeled shoes and tinted contact lenses, get tans, and have tummy tucks and facelifts. Even physical attributes are not immutable and fixed. In our culture, if a person wants to change, it is probably possible.

The physical facts are merely the start. Add a couple thousand other factors that make one unique: name, family of origin, friends and enemies, successes and failures. Some of the attributes that make us distinctive are clear to us and to everyone else. We are kind or cruel. We are fat or skinny. We are shy or bold. We are smart or ignorant. But some things about us are harder to name. What are we worried about? What makes us happy?

> "The unexamined life is not worth living."
>
> —SOCRATES

If you read my story and never get around to understanding your own story, then you have merely read parts of my memoir, which misses the point. My successes, failures, achievements, and addictions are probably not yours. The details and events of my life, while of vital importance to me, are merely illustrations of one person's long-term transformation. I lived by one set of habits and choices for a couple of decades, making decisions that were as natural as the air I breathed, and then I attempted to change some of them. You have to apply the principles of self-awareness and personal growth to your life. For example, I may talk too much, but you may talk too little. We likely have different challenges. The same principles and system I used to learn how to be quiet and listen better can help you speak up and communicate better. We all have life scripts (also known as "tapes," "maps," or "stories") that have led us to becoming who we are today. The challenge is to discover your life or family script. If you are sufficiently motivated to change, you will make an effort to transform yourself until you are the person you want to be.

> "What comes out of you when you are squeezed is what is inside of you."
>
> —WAYNE DYER

Nobody can fix you but you!

In counseling, the presenting issue is often not the underlying problem. I showed up at a therapist's doorstep, I thought, to help me learn how to cope with people who were angry with me. It did not take long for me to discover that my anger with them was a far more significant problem. Talking too much was another of my surface issues, but my more basic problem had to do with insecurity and the need to be liked. I felt the burden of entertaining whatever group I was in. Excessive credit card debt may be your symptom. What is the underlying problem? Why are you spending money you don't have? To keep up with the Joneses? Why is it important to keep up with them? Who are the Joneses anyway?

Where are you out of control? About which matters have you been told once too often that you have a problem? What do you suspect is an impediment in your life, even if no one else is aware of it? Too many pills? Your anger? Your finances? Your insecurity in relationships? Depression? Stubbornness? Fear of travel? A hobby that has become an obsession? Workaholism? Lack of communication with your children? Not enough time? Thoughts of suicide? Problems sleeping? Tobacco addiction? Nagging your spouse?

Part of the dilemma is that *you think you are normal.* We all believe other reasonable people feel (and should think and function) as we do. If you are a workaholic, you simply do not understand people who go home after an eight-hour workday or who don't labor through their lunch hour. Shouldn't everybody work as hard and as long as you do? The question, "What is wrong with them?" makes more sense to you than the question, "What is wrong with me?"

A life script or family script is an attitude or pattern of behavior learned in childhood. A life script is like water to a fish. Water is the world in which aquatic creatures live. If a fish could explain its surroundings, it might describe other fish, the seahorses, the shells on the ocean floor, the coral reefs, and the seaweed. But fish might take water for granted. That is the way scripts are. Weird behavior does not seem unreasonable to the person whose script says that behavior is normal. Thus, wife-beaters think all husbands abuse their spouses. Early in my career, when I worked with teenagers, I noticed that kids who used drugs typically thought that about 90 percent of the teenagers at their high school used drugs, while teenagers who did not use drugs would tell you that 90 percent of the kids were drug free. The truth was somewhere in between, but each group thought their world was *the* world.

Sometimes fixing problems is easy. You know something needs to be changed, so you change it. Sometimes overcoming obstacles seems almost impossible. You are not even sure what the issue is. In those circumstances, increased self-awareness is the place to start.

In counseling, I have always tried to help people determine what their family scripts are. Family scripts are varied: Always be courteous. Be a doctor. Be invisible. Be beautiful. Be feminine. Be poor. Be positive. Be powerful. Be rich. Be the star quarterback. Never cry. Children are to be seen and not heard. Clean your plate. Complain. Don't be late. Don't be powerful. Don't ever get angry. Don't ever let them see you sweat. Don't make good grades. Don't trust men. Don't trust rich people. Don't waste time. Don't worry; be happy. Eat dessert first. Go to church every Sunday. Have fun. If your

> "To see yourself as you really are is a greater miracle than raising the dead."
>
> —THE DESERT FATHERS

child has a temper tantrum in public, that means you are a bad parent. Intimidate people with whom you disagree. It's okay for husbands to hit wives. It's okay to lie. Life is hard. Make good grades. Marry a man you can control. Men are smarter than women. Men only want one thing. Always put fresh flowers on the table at dinner. Only Christians go to heaven. Only Muslims go to paradise. Our family always goes to the beach for vacation. The men in our family die young. The world is a frightening place. Wives are to submit to their husbands. Work first, then play. Worry about every-thing; don't be happy. You are irresponsible. You are not good enough. You are on your own. You are special. You can be anything you want to be. You can have anything you want. You can't have anything you want. You will be a good mother/father. You will be a terrible mother/father. Your sister is the good child; you are the bad child.

Figuring out your life scripts by yourself is a challenge. Sometimes they are obvious, but sometimes they are hidden. Sometimes they are positive and sometimes they are negative. I created this long list to indicate that there is no limit to how people are scripted. When I began my process of self-discov-ery, I wanted someone to show me a book that described the ten most common life scripts. No such volume exists because scripts are as diverse and as random as people are.

I am conscious that many people have unbearable pain in their past. They have events that wounded them far deeper than I am able to imagine. My effort to get people to do some basic, honest self-analysis by reflecting on various life events from their childhood may seem glib to those who have been raped, whose mothers were murdered, or who have lived in a wheel-chair since age five. I am in awe of people who have experienced life tragedies and are still in the process of working through and moving past such catastrophes. The goal is not to "get over" a horrific incident or circumstance any more than someone who has had an arm amputated "gets over" that. Arms don't self-regenerate, and neither do the parts of people's souls that suffer these tragedies.

> "Everybody agreed that, 'Yes, something happened to him when he was little, but I don't know what it was.'"
>
> —EDWARD HOAGLAND, *TIGERS AND ICE*

Still, I believe the principles for emo-tional, mental, and physical health remain the same, regardless of life's circumstances and surprises. Indeed, an almost certain path to a lifetime of depression, anger, and general chaos is the path of denial, of vengeance, or of com-pounding the first adversity by living as a victim and letting one characteristic become your defining feature. It is always telling to hear how people describe themselves, for good or ill: I am an amputee. I am a happily married man. I am a rape victim. I am a kindergarten teacher. I am a poor widow. I love to garden and play with my grandkids.

The most interesting people can't fit a self-description into a short sentence, positive or negative. You are a lot of things. I invite you to begin the process of thinking about your story and realizing what a truly remarkable person you are.

Have you ever seen a comparison between two prominent people (or even events) after a major tragedy? The first I remember was published after the assassination of John F. Kennedy. Suddenly, everywhere you looked, there were fascinating lists showing how many aspects of this event were similar to those surrounding the assassination of Abraham Lincoln. The names of Kennedy's and Lincoln's successors, Andrew Johnson and Lyndon Johnson, had the same number of letters in their first names and the same last name! Wow! Andrew Johnson was born in 1808 and Lyndon Johnson was born in 1908! What a coincidence! Each had two daughters! Unbelievable! This particular list named twenty-nine characteristics of Kennedy and Lincoln that were similar or identical. Is that amazing? No, it is not amazing or even unusual. Every human being, including you, has a couple of hundred thousand traits. I am sure you and I could find twenty-nine things that are identical or similar in the two of us. We could probably find hundreds if we looked long enough. Consider these:

> "Long experience has shown that when new information conflicts with our well-established preconceptions, it is either ignored, denied, or interpreted in such a way that our worldview remains intact."
>
> —GORDON LIVINGSTON, *AND NEVER STOP DANCING*

1. Your Physical Characteristics
   - Hair color?
   - Shoe size?
   - Broken bones or operations?
   - Tall or short? Fat or skinny? Curly or straight hair?
2. Your Parents
   - Names?
   - Occupations?
   - Ages at your birth?
   - Number of children?

- Names of children?
- Other descriptors?

3. Your Children
    - Number of daughters?
    - Number of sons?
    - Oldest daughter's name?
    - Youngest son's name?
    - Childhood diseases or accidents?

4. Your Personality
    - Favorite book?
    - Hobby?
    - Political party?
    - Favorite color?
    - Smoker or drinker?

Each of us has millions of descriptors that make us unique. DNA is just the beginning. Of course, people with too much time on their hands can find a couple of dozen things about any two of us that are surprisingly similar. Certainly there are odd happenstances. But, considering how incredibly complicated we are, it would be more of a fluke if two people could *not* find dozens of points of commonality. You and I are complex human beings with thousands of features and factors that make us who we are.

Each question can lead to forty other places to probe. "Script analysis" is a system of self-discovery that will last for the rest of your life, not the next hour of filling in blanks. What you see below is a condensed and free adaptation of questions therapists often ask on intake forms. This is not an adequate document for psychotherapeutic purposes but simply a beginning point for your journey to self-understanding. The difficulty in doing self-analysis is that we tend to recycle our old scripts. But thinking alone is better than not thinking at all! Who are you? What makes you unique? Ponder the questions and see what answers you discover.

> "The only way to do therapy with you is to study you."
>
> —PAUL CARLSON

## Self-Understanding

At some point in this process, you need to become more than a passive recipient of whatever insight and advice I offer. Keeping a journal will help. I am not referring to a "Dear Diary" chronicle in which you leave a record for your grandchildren of what you had for breakfast today, your current pet peeve, or which television programs you watched. Instead, I recommend journaling with a purpose. The first step of keeping a journal is to gather information and memories and to clarify your hopes. Then you will begin to move past a lack of self-awareness.

The questions below represent the kinds of queries a counselor or therapist might ask as she or he is getting to know you. There is an almost playful tone to this interrogation. If you were sitting in my office writing your answers, I would not want you somber and defensive. Give your first reactions. Have fun as you write your responses.

> "The market is flooded with surefire, easygoing formulas for a successful life that can be practiced in your spare time. Don't fall for that stuff, even though crowds of people *do*."
>
> —JESUS IN MATTHEW 7, PARAPHRASED BY EUGENE PETERSON IN *THE MESSAGE*

As always, there are a thousand other questions that could be asked in a thousand other ways, but these are some of the questions I ask. To a trained therapist, each answer leads to follow-up inquiries. In an appendix in this volume, I explain why I think these are important issues. Don't cheat and read the appendix until you have responded to the questions. Otherwise, you are trying to take an easy shortcut to a process that requires time, honesty, and effort. You can answer the questions below in a short sentence, a paragraph, or even several pages. Take your time. Enjoy the process.

## *Personal and Family History*

1. What is your name? Do you have nicknames? Who named you? Which of those names did you like and which did you dislike? Did you ever make an effort to change the name by which you were/are known?
2. What do you know about your conception and birth? Was there anything special, painful, wonderful, or otherwise significant about any part of your conception, your mother's pregnancy, labor, or delivery? Was any trauma involved? Were you wanted or unwanted?
3. Describe your parents when you were a child. Were they happy or depressed? Was life in your family a constant fight, or was it peaceful? Was

it boring? Describe your parents' marriage. Describe how they treated you. How did that compare to how they treated your siblings? What was the best thing about your parents? What was the worst thing about your parents?

4. Describe other relatives who were important in your family: brothers and sisters, aunt(s), uncle(s), grandparent(s), or others (even if unrelated) who lived with you for a period of time or to whom you were especially close. What was the best thing about each person? What was wrong with each person?

5. Name your family traditions. Are there any family stories or unusual events (these might go back several generations)? Is any ancestor well known, for good or ill? What did your family do on holidays?

6. What is your earliest childhood memory? Where did you live? With whom? Was there any kind of crisis in your family life when you were a child?

7. When you were in grade school, what was your favorite summer activity?

8. What was your favorite childhood game? What was your favorite childhood book or story? What subjects did you enjoy in school? What did you enjoy doing away from school? What was your favorite song as an adolescent? Who were your heroes and heroines? What was your favorite holiday? What was your hobby?

9. Describe a typical family meal. Who sat where at the table? Who cooked? Who cleaned? What were your favorite meals?

10. If you could change one thing about your childhood and adolescence, what would it be?

11. There are probably certain sentences that you could finish if your mom or dad (or primary caregiver) began to say them. Fill in the blanks as if that person were speaking:

Don't ever _____.
You are incapable of _____.
You should always _____.
You have no choice about _____.
Life is _____.
Be _____.

12. How have people in your family died? How do you expect to die? At what age?

13. What is your greatest disappointment in life thus far? What is your greatest success? What do you think you will be doing ten years from now if

things go badly? What do you think you will be doing ten years from now if things go well?

14. What would you like to give yourself permission to do?

# Chapter 7

# To Be Alive Is Power

Issue: *Empowerment*

Objective: I will enjoy being powerful and use my power constructively.

I was a young adult, immature, dumb, naïve, inexperienced, raw, unprepared for grownup reality. Somehow I had become the supervisor of another human being for the first time in my life, and I was in over my head. She was a bad employee and I was a bad boss. We didn't get along. She had an attitude and I was clueless. I talked to her about what I believed to be her deficiencies, and she told me what she believed to be my deficiencies. Being a religious person, I thought it was my duty to try to get along with this woman at least for a while, on her terms if necessary, even though I was the boss. Did I mention that I was stupid, foolish, and unwise? This impasse could not go on forever. I prayed that God would somehow move her to another community, that her husband would get transferred and take this woman out of my life. Her husband was not transferred and she stayed. She hunkered down and I whined to my wife and to anyone else who would listen about my difficult life at work. I felt helpless and hopeless . . . power-less. I dreaded going to my job every day. Why didn't God answer my prayers? Why didn't this woman go away? Wishing did not make it so!

Apparently, somewhere in my psyche I had enough chutzpah to suspect that my wish for something to be done would eventually require that I do something. No college education prepares you for the first time you have to terminate an employee. Eventually, I had to make a decision: was I going to do the job for which I was being paid a salary, or was I going to let this woman control my life and work? At that point in my life, firing that employee was the hardest thing I had ever done.

I did not die.

My life was not ruined.

She did not die, either, and her life was not ruined.

My parents had not prepared me for such challenges either. My dear, sweet, unassuming, powerless parents were salt-of-the-earth folks who accommodated themselves to others, never the reverse. They were undemanding and adapted themselves to the wishes of the more powerful people they encountered throughout their lives. As I got older, I dreaded seeing a salesperson walk through our door because my parents, poor as we were, could not say "No." They once bought a $600 alarm system for our tiny four-room house that was not worth $6000 at the time.

> "There is only one corner of the universe you can be certain of improving, and that is yourself."
>
> ——ALDOUS HUXLEY

I became what they modeled: easy-going, compliant, acquiescent, conforming, go-along and get-along, Mr. Congeniality. Some people rebel, but I was a good kid who never strayed far from what I was taught.

The trouble was that I had been taught one set of skills for getting through life. Reality requires multiple skill sets. Being accommodating, the ability I possessed, helped me get along with people, but when I attempted to get improved performance from an employee, being voted "Most Popular Boss" should not have been my goal.

The way you learn how to do hard things is by doing hard things. "I can't lose weight" will never lose weight. "I can't go back to school" will never go back to school. "I can't leave" will never leave a bad relationship. "I can't save money" will never save money. "I can't do something I have never done before" will never do anything new. Blazing new trails can be frightening, painful, and challenging. But new trails can be blazed. The impossible happens daily.

Power is morally neutral. Power can be used for noble causes, or it can be used to do harm. People rightly deplore the abuse of power by the powerful, but those who abdicate power by not appropriately asserting themselves have also abused power.

If the bullied, the wimpy, and the timid would stand up to the bullies, the power mongers, and the tyrants of the world, we would see more justice done. (The obvious corollary is that if the bullies, the power-mongers, and the tyrants behaved better, the world would be a better place, but I suspect that most people reading this volume are more likely to suffer from being disempowered than from being over-empowered. The sociopaths of the world do not think they need advice and rarely read self-help books.)

It has been said that when good people do nothing, evil prevails. Martin Luther King Jr., preached this theme as well as anyone: "Our lives begin to end the day we become silent about things that matter."

My presumption is that everyone with the ability to read this chapter is a person of some intrinsic power, even if that power is deeply buried and well hidden. Here is my story: I inherited a family and cultural script, taught to me by my parents and my church, that whispered to me daily, "Don't be powerful." That was in spite of being an intelligent, middle-class, able-bodied, heterosexual white male. I did not identify and articulate the nuances of this particular life map of powerlessness until I had been in the process of working on other scripts for several years. I knew I needed a fresh approach to some of my relationships. My life was not working out the way I wanted it to, and I felt vulnerable. With the help of a therapist, I defined a new goal: "I will enjoy being powerful and will use my power constructively."

There are three kinds of occurrences in the world: (1) those I control; (2) those someone else controls; (3) what I call "circumstances" (what insurance companies might call "acts of God"). A bumper sticker that reads, "Lead, follow, or get out of the way," approaches the spirit of what I am trying to say, though sound bytes rarely tell the whole truth. It is important to acknowledge that much of what happens in our lives is out of our personal control. I do not want to add to the pain in this world by "blaming the victims," by accusing them of not being smart enough or strong enough or aggressive enough to overcome the hurricane forces that blow through their lives. You and I cannot make our world a just place for people of all races and both genders and every economic strata any more than we can stop a hurricane from making landfall on the closest coastline. For instance, if you are born into the wrong caste in the nation of India or into poverty in Haiti, then pulling yourself up by your bootstraps is almost impossible. There are not enough self-help books available to provide certain people with the health, education, inspiration, encouragement, and family and cultural support they need to thrive and prosper. Someone with a different set of cultural givens may respond to the challenges of this volume and succeed in making significant positive changes in their lives. Not everyone is able-bodied and able-minded. Not everyone has equal access to the tools and opportunities required for self-improvement. I do not want to presume that every person who lives on this planet has access to what is necessary to create a full and satisfying life by altering, with the snap of a finger, the terrible cycles of poverty and powerlessness.

While some individuals need to fight to achieve new heights of empowerment at the personal level, others need to work to create more just societies where individuals with the will to succeed have that option available. If this were not a "self-help" volume, but were a treatise on the ethics of power, I would divide this chapter into two equal parts with these sub-headings: (1) Step Back and (2) Step Up.

> "There's bad folk everywhere, and what's far worse, weak ones."
>
> —ROBERT LOUIS STEVENSON, *KIDNAPPED*

The stepping back part is crucial for the just distribution of power. Some people are naturally dominant by virtue of being white, male, able-bodied, intelligent, wealthy, and/or scripted to be powerful within their cultures and families of origin. If they were to share some of their clout with those who are marginalized and disenfranchised by virtue of their race, gender, disability, IQ, poverty, and/or family script, that would make for a healthier, happier, more satisfying and peaceful world. If we never hear the voices of those outside the current hoarders of power, much less accommodate them, then the world will continue the cycle of favoring the already powerful and rebuffing those who are currently on the periphery. Thus, some people who possess power naturally need to *step back*.

Challenging the social structures of the world is beyond the scope of this book. In this volume I am concerned with creating newly empowered people more than altering inadequate infrastructures. Indeed, I am pleading for those who are able and who have the capacity to step up to accept the power that is rightfully theirs. If you think you are powerless to change, there will be no serious change in your life for the better.

I began my own assessment of power three decades ago during my doctoral work, thinking philosophically and globally about the ethics of power. Eventually I began to realize that ultimately I control only me. I do not have final jurisdiction for anyone else's personal decisions, including my wife, my parents, my workplace, my political representatives, my friends, even my own children over five years old. This insight is not a reason to stop attempting to influence others appropriately. I am not powerless. But I am a fool if I think I can control everything that goes on in the world around me.

This is a chapter about the authority and power I do have. *Step up.*

(Throughout this volume, I use a few words interchangeably that some scholars would rather I keep separate. Entire volumes have been composed describing the difference, at least in some researchers' minds, between "power" and "authority" or between "goals" and "objectives." However, I have written with the layperson in mind.

Machiavelli's *The Prince* is one of the most perceptive documents ever written about "power" from the point of view of a person desiring to wield power (c. 1513; repr., New York: St. Martin's Press, 1964). Machiavelli advises the "Prince" about how to prevail in any contest of wills. The flip side of Machiavelli's recommendations is that power can always be wielded against you. Machiavelli notes, "The deliberate action of a determined man [e.g., an assassin] cannot be avoided by princes, since anyone who does not fear death can himself inflict it." Assassins, of course, have changed the course of history. The Secret Service and special agencies that protect the president and the Pope are designed to defend the powerful from random acts of violence, but does anyone really believe the rich and the powerful are ultimately secure from an abrupt act of extreme hostility?

Power is a slippery thing. If I have to twist your arm, literally or metaphorically, to get you to make a decision or to do something I want you to do, then your decision and action will last only as long as I keep your arm twisted. How many scenes in movies have we witnessed when a captive finally gained her freedom, then immediately turned on her captor?

A dominant father can make his son sit down, and that father may think he has complete control of the situation, but the boy is thinking, "I may be sitting down on the outside, but I am standing up on the inside." Has the father really "won" that encounter?

"Our deepest fear is not that we are inadequate—our deepest fear is that we are powerful beyond measure. It is our light, not our darkness, that frightens us. We ask ourselves, 'Who am I to be so brilliant, gorgeous, talented and fabulous?' Actually, who are you not to be? You are a child of God."

—Nelson Mandela

I enjoy reading mystery and espionage novels because the heroes and heroines seem to know they always have options. Just when every door seems closed, they find a window. Just when every window seems shuttered, they hear a sound or feel a draft of frosty air that gives them a life-saving clue. You always have choices, but options do you no good if you are not aware of them.

One helpful technique I learned years ago in a workshop is what I began to call an "awareness exercise." (I have searched for its origins and found variations, but I cannot find the origin for this specific exercise.) The participant says, "I am aware that [insert a statement here of something observed or heard] and I take responsibility for that awareness." When I was counseling someone, I would demonstrate the exercise, and then ask the person in therapy to follow my lead. First, I gave examples of what I was currently aware of in the room where we were sitting. "I am aware that you are sitting on a black couch, and I take responsibility for that awareness." "I am aware of cars driving by on the street outside because I can hear them, and I take responsibility for that awareness." "I am aware that you are looking confused because your eyes are furrowed, and I take responsibility for that awareness." "I am aware that a light bulb in the lamp beside you has gone out, and I take responsibility for that awareness." "I am aware that the room is cold, and I take responsibility for that awareness." "I am aware that you still seem confused by what I am saying because your brow is wrinkled even more than it was, and I take responsibility for that awareness."

People often resisted the exercise because they resisted being aware and responsible for their awareness. The exercise may have seemed silly. But this simple tool, when I learned it, helped change my life! I think it can be helpful to others as well.

As a person who talked too much and listened too little, I was mostly unaware of my environment. A ringing phone could get my attention. An attractive female could get my attention. Yelling at me could get my attention. But I could go years without noticing the color of the drapes. Cluelessness did not make me a wicked person, but it did mean I was less in tune to my surroundings, including the people around me, than I might have been.

In counseling, as I taught this drill, I insisted that my clients say both parts of the sentence. They might say, "I am aware that you have a lot of books on your shelves, and I take responsibility for that awareness." "I am aware that I am also cold, and I take responsibility for that awareness." "I am aware that you are motioning me with your hands to keep on doing this exercise, and I take responsibility for that awareness."

The point of the exercise, when it is done correctly, is that at any given time we are aware of ninety-seven or one hundred and ninety-seven or even one thousand and ninety-seven different things simultaneously. Furthermore, new awarenesses quickly tumble into our consciousness (or unconsciousness) on top of each other. We perceive light, colors, and other visual stimuli, smells, heat and cold, body pain, noises—all at the same time! Something in our system sorts through this barrage of information and declares, "This one is important and that one is not important." If our systems did not do that, we would live under more stress than we could bear. Our sorting mechanisms come from a host of directions, and some of them may be compromised! Is there a pea under the mattress, or a cantaloupe, or nothing? Is there a smell of something burning in the house or not? Are you merely looking at me, or are you glaring at me, or are you laughing at me, or are you thinking of someone else you talked to earlier today?

> "You get treated in life the way you teach people to treat you."
>
> —WAYNE DYER

Of course, the ultimate goal of this exercise is not to make sure we know the temperature of the room or the color of the paint on the wall, but to make us aware of the far more subtle clues about life that we often miss even though they are right in front of us.

Sometimes, in a counseling session, someone would say the phrase incorrectly. I am not ordinarily a stickler for detail, but I insisted that the person get this drill right. One might say, "I am aware that you have a lot of books stacked high on your desk, and I am responsible for that."

*No!* How could you be responsible for the number of books I have in my office? You are *not* responsible for anything in my office except for yourself. You are responsible for being aware of my clutter, but you are not responsible for my clutter! If my books are piled precariously, you should not lean on them. If there is a loaded mousetrap on top of one stack of books, you need to keep your hands to yourself. You are not responsible for any of my habits, words, or actions. You are only responsible for your own awareness and your responses. Be honest. Be thorough. What do you see? What do you hear? What do you smell? Are you paying attention?

You are responsible for what you say and what you do after you become aware. No wonder people enjoy being clueless. No wonder people like to say, "I had no idea." No wonder people resist knowledge. No wonder being dumb is such an attractive option. When you say, "I did not know," then you believe you got off the responsibility hook. If you could not have known, you are indeed absolved of guilt, blame, or responsibility. But if you could have known, if you could have paid attention better, then your ignorance is an inadequate excuse.

At some point in a person's pilgrimage, words and thoughts need to give way to action. The world is full of wannabes who believe every word of enlightenment and encouragement they read or hear, but they never act on those words! They are morally impotent. Too often I have known people who seemed to agree with every word of wisdom anybody uttered, but when a crisis appeared, they caved in to old habits. When difficulty arose, they fell back on deep-rooted and predictable routines. They blamed. They whined. They acted as if not a single word of wisdom or advice they heard made any difference to them. Good intentions are worthless. You must understand that you are responsible for your own life; you have enough power to make the changes you need to make. But *you* must *do* something. *You* must take some transformational action. *You* have work to do. This chapter is about *your power.* If you walk away with more information but are no more empowered to assume control over your life, then you have missed the point and missed your opportunity.

Power can be positive. Being empowered means you can actually do something if you choose to do it! Your options may seem limited, but most of us can act in some small way. We can turn off the television. We can leave the room. Power over a hurricane may mean evacuating. An ancient puzzle asks, "How do you walk through a wall?" The answer? "Build a door."

> "Some people seem to be afraid of success. Do they think failure is better than success? After all, those are the two options."
>
> —EARL CRAIG

My friends who are community organizers say power equals the *willingness* plus the *ability* plus the *capacity* to act. If you see a box on the ground, you have the power to lift it if (a) you desire to lift it (willingness), (b) you are physically able to lift it (ability), and (c) your hands are free (capacity).

But if I feel powerless, and I accept my powerlessness as a fact, then I comply helplessly with any and all consequences: "I am fat because my wife cooks fattening meals." "I am poor because my parents were poor." "I am unhappy because . . . ." "I was late because . . . ."

An emotionally healthy person can always choose to give up power, but being empowered must precede this decision. That was an enormously important insight for me. Having been raised in my parents' home, my default position was powerlessness. I gave in instinctively. As I began to get healthier emotionally, I discovered other options regarding power. Indeed, as I became more aware of how power relationships work, I discovered that what is disempowering to one person or group of people is usually not good for others either. To do for someone what they can do for themselves is often disempowering to the person we think we are helping.

When I was in college, one of the battles that raged between the students and the administration fell under the rubric *in loco parentis*. The administration believed curfews (midnight for men and nine o'clock p.m. for women) protected the young innocents who had been placed "in their care." But college students rebelled against such authority, especially against the unsympathetic decision makers who wanted to tell them when to go to bed. These young men and women had left Mom and Dad behind at home and didn't want the dean to take their parents' place. Protecting people who don't want or need to be protected may be more disempowering and unkind than it seems at first.

Exerting power over people unnecessarily is rarely a good thing for the powerbroker either. The goal is to use your power for the benefit of both yourself and others. Ironically, the assumption of too much power can sometimes make the powerful powerless. Some citizens do not seem inhibited by the constraints of their childhood or even by the laws of society. They don't need more power. Their lack of control is the result of too much power. At Riverside Church in New York City, I once heard William Sloane Coffin explain how power progresses and then regresses: "Powerful, more powerful, most powerful, powerless." The individual who feels like he or she can do "everything" may end up incarcerated, unable to do "anything." Everyone's issues are not the same. Some people need to *step back*, and some need to *step up*.

One of the realities of our world is that the prosperous and powerful have always found a way to get the working classes—the people who make their money for them—to believe that their hard labor is for their own benefit. The American Civil War and the Post-Reconstruction era are classic examples. While the war was clearly about slavery, the plantation owners "spun" the conflict as being about "states' rights." A man who owned no slaves would hardly want to sacrifice his life in battle merely so the slave owners could keep getting wealthier. But if the poor family was convinced that the evil people in Washington and farther north were trying to steal something from them, then even non-slave owners would volunteer to fight! I've seen it in sports. I've seen it in big business. People want to make a profit for themselves. There is nothing inherently wrong with that. The glitch comes when either the powerful or the powerless believes an unreal fantasy. An emotionally and intellectually healthy person will try to move past the "spin" or "packaging" and understand the whole truth.

The United States of America is an open society thanks to freedoms of religion, speech, press, and peaceful assembly—all guaranteed in the First Amendment to the Constitution. We should also thank newspapers, radio, television, cheap travel, and, nowadays, the Internet. In fact, everywhere in the world, the truth has become more difficult to hide. One reason the Berlin Wall and the old Soviet Union fell was because the truth could not be squelched forever. In *The World Is Flat* (New York: Farrar, Straus, and Giroux, 2007), Thomas L. Friedman argues convincingly that the barriers that once restricted the flow of information have been effectively overcome in the twenty-first century. Almost everyone who wants information has access to it. Over the Internet, minorities, women, the disabled, and even geeky teenagers are now finding success.

I finished high school as a member of the infamous "Class of '65" that got caught between the old system of trusting the authorities and the new wave of "doing your own thing." We learned that just because people were in positions of power did not mean they were right. If bullets could not win the day, maybe flowers would. I am an almost perfect example of the ambivalence of my generation. I am a loyal, traditional kind of fellow, a patriot, a compliant conservative in many ways and a progressive, a liberal, and a rebellious free spirit in others. As an adult, I am unimpressed by the argument, "We've never done it that way before," and I am equally unimpressed by anarchy. I am as unmoved by a posturing liberal political candidate as I am by a knee-jerk conservative. No political party has my best interests at heart, and you and I are fools to believe that anybody with money and power and fame is truly looking out for me better than I am able to look after myself. But I am not a cynic. I believe there are good people in government, in business, in religion, and in the press, and I believe many of our best institutions have created trustworthy systems with appropriate checks and balances. Still, no organization is guaranteed to be good forever. Accountability of the powerful and empowerment of the powerless are equally necessary both in times of community crisis and every day of the week.

This was not an overnight revelation to me. It took me years to come to this conclusion. As a child, I learned a Bible verse that read, "Bear one another's burdens" (Gal 6:2). It is a short, memorable, and lovely sentiment. When you have a basic need, a burden, I should attempt to help you. What was not taught to me was a Bible verse only two sentences later: "Bear your own burdens" (Gal 6:5). Why was that passage of Holy Scripture not also emphasized? Both are important. I am responsible for myself. There is no need for your family to go out and buy groceries for my family when we are capable of buying our own. Do you know I like asparagus? Raspberries? Red snapper? Oysters? Do you know I use fat-free cream in my coffee? Of course you know none of that, and I don't know what you like, so it makes perfect sense for you to go out and buy your own groceries and for me to buy my own groceries. Ordinarily, each person bears his or her own burdens. Sometimes, though, unfortunate things happen, and there are times when one of us needs help. If my family or your family is distressed beyond our ability to care for ourselves, then it makes sense for one of us to help the other out. Bear one another's burdens.

> "Don't be afraid to take a big step if one is indicated. You can't cross a chasm in two small jumps."
>
> —DAVID LLOYD GEORGE

Under most circumstances, I am responsible for myself. If my life is going to be improved, it will usually be me who improves it. One of my primary doctoral projects was on "The Just Use of Power." As I have already stated, power is morally neutral, just like dynamite, money, and chewing gum. The ethics question is, "What do you do with your power?" If you run into the street and pick up a two-year-old child when a car is coming toward her, then you have used power for a moral good. If you shove that same two-year-old child in front of that same car, you have used your might for a moral evil.

My contention is that the "Just War Theory," a system used by people who care about the ethical dimensions of international relationships, is also a good structure to help us reflect on the moral use of power in other contexts. There are many ancient and modern sources for the Just War Theory, but I include the following components:

1. There must be a *just cause.* "Because I want what you have" is not sufficient cause for nations or individuals to overpower (or conquer or suppress) others.

2. There must be a *just intention.* It is possible to have a just cause but an unjust intention. Your enemy (or your nation's enemy) did something wrong, and your leaders determine it is appropriate to use power to address that wrong, but then they also decide to add a bit of vengeance to the response. They will not simply get back what was taken, but they also decide to destroy the enemy nation's infrastructure. Their intention is neither honorable nor just.

3. The act of war or the use of overwhelming power must be a *last resort.* Have all other means been used to achieve the desired end? It is not good for a caregiver to preempt the response of another person, keeping him or her in a position of dependency. In reading a book by Carmen Renee Berry called *When Helping You Is Hurting Me* (New York: Crossroad Publishing Co., 2003), I became convinced that intervening too early or too often sounds like a much kinder act than it actually is; rather than helping, it implies the incompetence of the other.

4. There must be a *clear announcement of the intention* to go to war or to assert your power.

5. There must be a *reasonable hope of success.* You have done no one any good and have not acted ethically if you attempt to do something that is doomed to failure.

6. There must be a *just authority.* How many times have power-hungry individuals usurped authority that was not theirs to have? "I think you should resign before the boss fires you." "If it were me, I would tell her no." "You ought to give him the money." What is the standing of the third party in a particular situation? Who gave her or him authority to act or make a decision or even a suggestion? In unhealthy relationships, this is a serious problem as people create complicated relationship triangles.

Admittedly, a "Just Power Theory" is too much to think about every time you are trying to decide whether or not to eat a particular candy bar or go on a date or work late. But you learn how to do something by practicing it. Start somewhere, anywhere, and learn how to use power justly and ethically.

In my analysis of the ethical dimensions of the use of power, I argue for accountability as the key issue. Utter independence and absolute autonomy are rarely good things. If you own the business, then it is certainly within your power to terminate an untenured employee without an investigation. But words such as "due process," "consensus," and "collaboration" have become essential in our culture for good reason. At the very least, I hope for the humility of being aware that there is more than one point of view to any situation. The goal is not to become an obstructionist, stopping life for a lengthy six-point analysis every time a minor decision is made. The goal is to have the right tools available when they are needed.

Over the past thirty years, I have made hundreds of difficult decisions, from admitting my mother to a hospital against her will to putting my beautiful dog Prissy to sleep. I do not pretend that I have become comfortable with making difficult decisions. But, for the most part, I now do what needs to be done, even when it involves risk and pain.

# Chapter 8

# Five Models of Maturity

Issue: *Roots and Wings*

Objective: I will grow to my potential.

## Five Models of Maturity

Numerous systems of understanding emotional growth and maturity have enjoyed their fifteen minutes or fifteen years of fame. They vary considerably in style and emphasis, and each speaks of attaining maturity in different ways. As a layman, when it comes to the intricacies of psychiatry and psychology, I have no particular expertise. Nonetheless, I have learned much from each of the approaches below. I present them in random order because no one system has the whole truth, any more than one food group has all the vitamins, minerals, and nutrition we need for good physical health.

> "I was seventeen, and knew it all, My dreams were big, But my thoughts were small."
>
> —"JESUS AND MAMA" BY CONFEDERATE RAILROAD

### Eric Berne: Transactional Analysis

Eric Berne contends, and I agree with him, that every human relationship involves a transaction of some sort. If I go to the coffee shop, I give the waitress money and she gives me coffee. We have had a successful transaction. If the transaction has been a fair one, I am happy with my coffee, she is happy with her wage and my tip, and the coffee shop owner is happy with a small profit. If I asked that coffee shop clerk out on a date, and she accepted, then another type of transaction has happened. We "spend" time with each other in hopes of a "payoff." This transaction isn't as contractually clear as the purchase of coffee, but it is an exchange nonetheless, a social "contract" if not a monetary one. For the "investment" of a couple of hours, we may make a new friend, acquire a lover, or discover a lifelong partner. A transaction occurs. If that first "exchange" away from the coffee shop went well, we may repeat it and go out again, and even again, until one of us feels that there is no longer "value" in the arrangement.

> "The brain functions as a high-fidelity recorder, putting on tape, as it were, every experience from the time of birth, possibly even before birth."
>
> —THOMAS A. HARRIS, *I'M OK, YOU'RE OK*

If there is no possibility of a payoff, a reasonable exchange, then we don't engage in the transaction. Under ordinary circumstances, if a fifty-year-old married man asks that same teenage waitress out on a date, she will decline. There is no obvious inducement for her. She doesn't want him for a lover, a marriage partner, or even a friend. She will say "no" if he has been bold enough to ask. Certain realities can change the equation, even in this scenario. If the fifty-year-old man is Donald Trump (or someone equally wealthy), Sean Connery (or someone equally famous), or Bill Clinton (or someone equally powerful), then possibly the teenage girl will accept the "date." Or, if the man is the waitress's roommate's dad who is in town for a business meeting, and her roommate happens to be out of town, she may agree to have lunch with him as a favor to her on this one occasion. She "owes" that to her roommate. We act for particular reasons, even if those reasons are not obvious or make no sense to anyone else or even to ourselves.

If you do something, there is a payoff. Period. You may have never thought about what the payoff is, but there is an incentive. Every human encounter that involves anything more than two people merely brushing past one another is a transaction that can be analyzed. You can conduct a "transactional analysis."

In his system, Berne divides the human personality into three components: the *parent*, the *adult*, and the *child*.

The parent part of our personalities reflects what we were taught by (or what we "caught from") the authority figures in our young lives. These were probably our parents, unless grandparents or guardians raised us. Teachers, rabbis, priests, preachers, and older siblings can also fill this role. Who do you hear when someone points a finger at you and shakes it in your face, telling you what to do or what not to do? Conversely, who took care of you and nurtured you as a child? Who let you sleep with them when you were sick? You don't have to be a parent to encounter the parent part of your psyche. Watch any five-year-old playing with dolls, and you will see her point her fingers and scold. You will also see her warmly embrace her favorite dolls to provide nurture and comfort.

The child part of our personalities is what we feel when that finger points toward us and/or a voice raises at us in anger. We cringe fearfully. The child is also the part of our personalities that enjoys laughing and playing and being free of care because someone else is taking care of us.

The adult is the third part of our personalities, which emerges when we are rational and in control of the circumstances in which we find ourselves. You might think the goal is always to be adult. You would be wrong. If you have school-aged children, then you need to parent your offspring, not befriend them. They don't need their parents to be their peers or their pals. They need parents. A teacher in a classroom needs to have authority. A manager in a crisis needs to be assertive, to take charge. There are times when putting on your "parent" hat is a good thing.

The same is true of the child portion of your persona. Even as mature adults, there is a time to be free of care. When I go to a sports game, that is a play day for me. I don't want to work. I don't want to be responsible for anything. When I am sick and need to be in bed under someone else's

> "Games are passed on from generation to generation. The favored game of any individual can be traced back to his parents and grandparents, and forward to his children; they in turn, unless there is a successful intervention, will teach them to their grandchildren . . . ."
>
> —ERIC BERNE, *GAMES PEOPLE PLAY*

care, then I am willing to submit to their tender ministrations. I don't always need to be in control. There are times when it is okay to be a child. So-called "intellectuals" can sometimes make themselves and their significant others miserable by turning every human encounter into a thoughtful, fully considered, rational, "adult" exchange. There is a time when it is okay to play and to relax. I don't have to teach my adult daughters or my grandson an important life lesson every time we spend thirty minutes together. We can simply enjoy a game of Hearts or laugh at a TV sitcom. We can simply go to an Easter egg hunt and revel in the joy and exuberance of the event. Must I always be a rational, level-headed, boring adult? I hope not. Every hour of every day should not be deadly dull! There needs to be time for play. With those caveats, I would argue that adults ordinarily ought to function as adults in relationship to other adults.

The parent/adult/child relationship is drawn as a diagram of stacked circles:

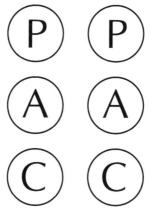

For a transaction to occur, and for it to be analyzed, at least two people must be involved. As you read this, you and I are (probably) having an adult-to-adult transaction. You were willing to spend your money on this book, or to spend your time going to the library to check it out, because you hoped there would be a payoff, something beneficial to you. You want to receive something for your time, money, and effort. Likewise, I have made the investment of my time to write this book (getting up early on Saturday mornings, for example) because I anticipate receiving royalties. Also, and maybe more important, it is satisfying to me to help people. In this transaction, we both give something, and each of us receives something.

If, however, your boss said you must read this volume to keep your job, and you must make a written report on it and turn it in on Monday morning, then it is possible that I seem to you like an overbearing and arrogant parent (or teacher or some other authority figure). If that is the case, then you will read every word of this volume as if you were a dominated child.

Transactional analysis can become sophisticated. For example, the parent can have two contrasting components: (1) the critical parent, the authority figure who scolds and disciplines, or (2) the nurturing parent, the comforting individual who praises and protects.

The child, likewise, can respond to life situations in two contrary ways: (1) the okay child, the carefree, blessed person who is relaxed, or (2) the not okay child who is uptight, anxious, and feels cornered, blamed, and under attack.

My goal is not to give you a detailed understanding of transactional analysis in these few sentences, but to introduce you to a system of understanding human relationships that takes seriously the differences in the behavior of adults and children. Thirty- and forty-year-old individuals who act as if they were still ten, cowering at the sound of a raised voice, need to grow up.

## Rabbi Edwin Friedman: Family Systems Theory

Family systems theory also seeks to understand human development and maturity by analyzing relationships. It asks, "What has gone on and what is going in the life of the extended family?" In other words, an adult son may not reach full maturity, even though he is sixty years old, until his domineering father, the patriarch of the family, dies. By dying, Dad finally allows his compliant and seemingly powerless son to become the mature adult he has never been allowed to be while the dominant dad was still alive. Murray Bowen and Ed Friedman are the two gurus of this movement. As a pastor, I was introduced to this organic understanding of human growth by Rabbi Friedman, whose book, *Generation to Generation* (New York: Guilford Press, 1985), is helpful for understanding human organizations and relationships.

Several words are important in family systems theory.

*Homeostasis* and *symmetry* describe the desire for balance within a family, business, or social system. As long as a family, an organization, or even an entire culture seems to be working adequately, it will resist changing from its current course. There is nothing surprising in that statement. Communities have always ostracized those who challenge the status quo and advocate change. If a child asserts himself or herself in a new way, the rest of the family or organization often shuts out that person and/or discounts them as a troublemaker, a rabble rouser, the wild child, the radical. In the Hebrew Bible, consider the story of Jacob and his twelve sons. The favored son named Joseph, with his attention-grabbing coat of many colors, could not fulfill his destiny in the dysfunctional family system in which the manipulative father dominated his wives, concubines, and all his sons and daughters. To be *self-differentiated*, Joseph needed to live in an entirely different country. Even after he ended up in Egypt, changing history there, the other eleven sons continued to be bullied by their father and were unable to make a free and independent decision for the good of the family. Every decision had to go through Dad. These "boys" were still acting like frightened six-year-old kids, overwhelmed

> "Whatever we are struggling with has its legacy in the struggles of prior generations. If we do not know about our own family history, we are more likely to repeat past patterns or mindlessly rebel against them, without much clarity about who we really are, how we are similar to and different from other family members, and how we might best proceed in our own life."
>
> —HARRIET G. LERNER,
> *THE DANCE OF ANGER*

and overpowered by their father. They never grew up. Nobody was up to the task of challenging Father Jacob. Homeostasis reigned! That is a fancy way of saying everything stayed the same and life was static! No changes. No challenges. A lot of unhappy people.

Rabbi Friedman argues that when circumstances finally change as a result of death or disability, the "system" will work to right itself as quickly as feasible, unsettling itself as little as possible. Somebody always assumes power. The more stable the family system (or organization or government), the less volatile the change. If there is an "heir apparent," and he or she assumes the literal or figurative throne unchallenged, there is little disruption in the system. If, on the other hand, a civil war is needed to determine the next king or queen, patriarch or matriarch, CEO or president, then there is great upheaval. Homeostasis is lost. The symmetry of the equation is lost. Injustice is alleged. One person or "side" believes they now have less power than they need or deserve. They are willing to do whatever it takes to restore equilibrium as they define it, even if great turmoil results. What one person perceives as "balance" and social "stability" appears to be an inflexible system to another. What one person perceives as positive change and growth toward maturity is seen as a frightening cause for panic to another. These upheavals happen every day in families, synagogues, law offices, medical practices, schools, churches, businesses, and governments.

Sometimes these developments are obvious. Sometimes they are subtle. I have seen surprising events take place after the death of a parent. Sometimes they don't appear to involve a power struggle. But when an unmarried fifty-year-old woman with three children gets married for the first time only six months after her father dies, an attentive observer would be suspicious that something besides a wedding is taking place. Some old score is being settled. Some inequity is being fixed. I may not be sure what, and neither may the person getting married, but something is happening. When a seventy-year-old man whose mother just died presents himself for baptism two weeks later, some new imbalance in the family system is being adjusted or corrected.

Watch what happens after a major life transition in a family. Almost immediately, other major events follow. Someone gets pregnant. Someone moves far away. Some family member returns to live nearby or even comes back to the family home. Someone does something to get arrested. Someone gets divorced. One family member grows up. Another who has seemed independent now wants to be taken care of. Someone is in a serious accident. One change begets other changes. You can bet on it. This principle works in families, businesses, synagogues, churches, partnerships, governments, and sports teams.

Family systems theory is a reminder that life is tangled and that we are more interdependent than we think we are. Growth toward maturity requires some independence, some self-differentiation, from family, religious, business, and other loyalties that keep us stuck in old habits and patterns.

## Scott Peck: Moral Growth and Development

Years ago, I heard Scott Peck lecture in Columbia, South Carolina, regarding what he called "categories of religious thought." These paragraphs are gleaned from notes I took at his lecture, so any deficiencies in this outline are mine, not his. If I heard him correctly, he said there are four stages of moral development.

He labeled the first stage *Chaotic and Antisocial.* These are the hedonists, narcissists, and sociopaths, those who believe they are the center of the known universe. Their theme is "It's all about me." Leave the world to them, and there is anarchy. These people are unprincipled and unwilling to do the work that love or justice requires. It may never occur to them that being kind to other people is something they might want to consider—unless doing a good deed promotes their own agenda.

"It just can't go on like this, boss; either the world will have to get smaller or I shall have to get bigger."

—NIKOS KAZANTZAKIS, *ZORBA THE GREEK*

The second stage is what Peck called the *Formal and Institutional* level of moral development. These are people who understand the need to submit to authority. Many individuals who are disorderly outside a structured environment end up thriving within a regulated organizational structure, such as a prison or the military or a fundamentalist sect. People who function at this level also perform well in a structured business environment where they are told when to be at work, what kind of clothes to wear, what to do when they get there, and exactly how to do their jobs. They also gravitate to churches or mosques where they are told what to believe, how to live, how much to give, which secular activities to embrace, and which to avoid. Conversion from the chaos of stage 1 to the structure of stage 2 is a joyful conversion. Ask any alcoholic who has gotten sober. Ask any criminal who has quit a life of crime. This is a glorious time for the convert and his or her family. Even at this stage of moral growth, it is still mostly about the individual's good feelings. The person may evangelize or send money to missionaries so other people will experience the same insights and changes, but his or her own values and experiences are the norms by which all others are judged. "You shouldn't drink beer because beer made me drunk, and I did bad things when I was drunk." "You should go to mass because I stopped beating my wife and kids when I started going to mass." These folks desire for their lives to be better. Simple, easily understood commandments help them achieve their goals: Don't steal. Don't curse. Don't drink alcoholic beverages. Don't gamble. Go to church on Sunday. They prefer for life to get no more complicated than that. Many religious people never move beyond stage 2 in their growth.

Some religious people as well as many agnostics and atheists are at stage 3, because it is the *Skeptical and Individual* stage. Peck believes these people, even the irreligious ones, are often more spiritually developed than the churchgoers in stage 2. They desire to be good parents. They want to be kind and loving. They are truth-seekers. They work out their own faith system (or lack thereof) as individuals and resist groupthink. Many skeptics reject the church because they do not respect the thoughtless immaturity and the blind obedience they see in certain religious groups. They might like Jesus or Mohammed if they could get past the excessive cultural baggage converts seem to be required to carry.

Conversion to stage 3 is usually painful because it almost always means leaving behind some of your childhood jingles, myths, rules, and values. It is time to start over. Throw out the old that no longer makes sense and build a life that does. Peck's argument, and I agree with him, is that emotional and moral growth do not occur until a person is able to move past the predictable and facile answers a child is expected to give. Until they discover truth on their own, they make no serious progress toward being adults. There is an old joke about a pastor who was leading a "children's sermon" one Sunday. He asked the children if they knew what was furry, climbed trees, and ate nuts. One of the precocious youngsters said, "Reverend, I know the answer is always supposed to be God, but it sure sounds like a squirrel to me." The morally mature are able to recognize a squirrel when they hear one described.

The final stage in Peck's understanding of moral growth is the *Mystical and Transpersonal* category. People in this arena understand that the world is bigger than the categories of their childhoods, larger than the geographic region of their births, greater than the culture of their forebears, and more inclusive than the religion of their parents. They thrive on mystery and value grace. Peck got a big laugh in his lecture when he guessed that everyone in his audience surely saw themselves at stage 4. Conversion to stage 4 from stage 3 is most often incremental rather than dramatic.

Peck did not say this, but I suspect many of those who think they are at stage 4 are simply stuck in stage 3 or may have even recycled their way back to stage 2. With good minds and good educations, they learned new ideas, assumed they were liberated from the restrictions of their past, and became members of an elite intelligentsia. But it seems that many of these people have simply substituted a new intolerance for the old intolerance. Rejecting the fundamentalism and legalism of their

> "I'd come to the end of all I knew."
>
> —LEAH PRICE AFTER HER SISTER'S DEATH IN *THE POISONWOOD BIBLE* BY BARBARA KINGSOLVER

childhood culture or religion, they now embrace a new gracelessness for those who are not as enlightened as they believe they are. True stage-4 men and women would have, I think, a bit more grace for those who are stuck at a "lower" level of maturity, wishing better for them. I know many so-called "liberals" (those who believe they are liberated and free) who are just as rigid and uncompromising as "conservatives" and "fundamentalists."

People are always threatened by those in the "higher" stages. People in stage 1 are in terror of everyone. People in stage 2 (the inflexible) are contemptuous of those in stage 1 and clueless about the people in stages 3 and 4. Men and women in stage 3 are often condescending and disdainful toward those in stages 1 and 2, but aren't yet willing to embrace the full mystery of level 4. They would rather play the role of resident radical or sophomore cynic. The challenge of level 4 is to incorporate all levels of human functioning into an understanding of life without harsh judgment toward those who do not and maybe never will "get it."

## Sigmund Freud: The Id, the Ego, and the Superego

Sigmund Freud describes three aspects of the maturing individual. First, there is the *id.* The id is the part of us that eats, fights, demands, grabs, desires sex, poops, passes gas, and pretty much wants what it wants when it wants it, craving instant gratification. Obviously, this id component is alive and well from the instant of our birth. No time or maturity is required to develop the id. At the opposite end of the spectrum is the *superego,* the transcendent ("bigger than I") morals and values taught us by our parents and our culture—what we should do and what we should not do. Chronologically, the superego is developed in our earliest years of childhood. Parents, teachers, preachers, big sisters and brothers, aunts and uncles, and other caregivers instruct and punish us for what they believe to be our misbehavior, for hitting, for taking what is not ours, for pooping in our pants, for playing with our private parts in public. The superego tells us to share a limited supply of food, to restrain our various impulses, eventually including our desire to have indiscriminate sex, and to avoid passing gas in public. The superego embodies the rules by which we have been instructed to live; it desires perfection. The superego is emphatic: go, do, stop, hurry, never, always, now! We become fearful and anxious of doing what we have been taught not to do, and we feel guilty if we do it. The superego keeps us from acting like barnyard animals, raping and pillaging

> "Disclose us to ourselves."
>
> —KAHLIL GIBRAN, *THE PROPHET*

our way through life. The superego, however, can be just as mindless and thoughtless as the id. While some adults walk around functioning as infants, saying, "I want what I want when I want it," others live in habitual fear of making Mom and Dad (or God) angry, saying, "I must not, I should not, I ought not." They also seem never to develop fully emotionally.

The *ego* (the I) is the rational part of the human psyche. The ego thinks. The ego takes into account both the desire and the restraint and makes a rational decision about what is the best course of action. The ego can say yes to the id, or it can say yes to the superego, or it can assess multiple options with appropriate maturity and choose a compromise. The ego, when it is mature and developed, seeks to function in a suitable fashion, grieving when grieving is fitting, laughing when laughing makes sense, and eating when eating is proper. Even though Mom and Dad taught us to use a toilet when we need to urinate or defecate, as mature individuals, our egos can assess the circumstances in which we find ourselves, make an adult decision, and go behind the nearest tree if we so choose.

> "For in Freudian theory, the superego is not just a voice; it is an operator, a subtle and complex manipulator, a prover of points. It prosecutes, judges, and carries out sentences, and it does all this quite outside of our conscious awareness."
>
> —MARTHA STOUT, *THE SOCIOPATH NEXT DOOR*

## Erik Erikson: Identity and the Life Cycle

Erik Erikson delineates eight stages of human development from birth to death.

1. *Infants, birth to 12 to18 months.* The earliest basic life conflict Erikson says we must resolve is *trust versus mistrust.* If a child does not begin to answer the question about whom and what is trustworthy, the individual will be permanently confused (dysfunctional) when he or she moves outside the home environment in later years. Some people may suppose, as I once did, that the task of the child is only to learn how to trust. However, learning whom and when to mistrust are equally important. A crawling baby must learn that a hot stove or fire or snarling dog is not harmless. On the one

hand, if nothing is trustworthy, that is a problem. Children must learn to feel safe. On the other hand, if parents are overprotective, always responding even before the child can feel the slightest pain, then naïveté and gullibility may result. At the earliest stage, infants begin to learn, for good or ill, about the basic life issue of trust and mistrust.

"All the babies who are smiled at and hugged will know how to love. Spread these virtues throughout the world; nothing else need be done."

2. *Toddlers, ages 18 months to 3 years.* The life task of this age, according to Erikson, has to do with *autonomy versus shame and doubt.* Improving physical skills is the child's growth goal at this age. Thus, control of the muscles is the prime example of success, particularly walking and using the toilet. When a child is able to do these things, he or she can be successfully autonomous in significant ways. Alternatively, in some homes, parents have gone overboard in affirming and overprotecting their children. The goal of parents whose children are in the "terrible twos" is to teach them that they are not God! For the first portion of their needy little lives, babies are the center of attention. Everything must be done for them. They cry and the parent responds. That must change as a child gets older. Toddlers, older children, and certainly adults should not get every toy they want, every food they desire, or all the attention they crave. Occasionally not getting your way is a part of life.

3. *Preschoolers, ages 3 to 6 years.* Erikson says that at this stage, the work that eventually leads to complete maturity has to do with *initiative versus guilt.* There are similarities in this and the previous stage. A toddler may not know that you should not flush a diamond bracelet down a toilet, but a five-year-old should know better. All kinds of meanness can result when children or adults think they can do whatever they want, wherever they want, whenever they want. On the other hand, if guilt is the overwhelming childhood emotion, then there is too much fear and too little initiative. Inappropriate inhibitions can result when children think whatever they do is wrong. They reason, "Better to do nothing than to do something and be wrong." If someone shuts down at the first sign of criticism from his new boss, I suspect he or she had a childhood home in which mistakes were not tolerated.

4. *School age, ages 7 to 12 years.* According to Erikson, this is the age when children establish a work ethic, the task being *industry versus inferiority.* In some ways, this stage is more of the same, but the community imposing the values keeps getting larger. Up until now, the family, primarily the parents, has provided the norms by which the child has lived. If a daughter could get away with being the queen of her household, then that is what she did. Now the community gets involved, particularly the school and neighborhood. The school-aged child discovers that the class has several other queens and a few kings as well. These roles are validated or challenged. One of the young girls who thought she was a queen may discover that she is no more special than other children, and in fact she may be ordinary, not as smart, not as pretty, and not as ambitious. Someone who has lived more or less battered by a horrible home life may find new energy. The hard work that got no rewards at home is prized at school. The world is full of testimonies of how one teacher or coach or organization helped make a life-changing difference in the destiny of one child. Unfortunately, many people became stuck (what Erikson calls "inertia") in their maturing process, permanently feeling inferior. They carry into adulthood a self-understanding of themselves as incompetent.

5. *Teen years, ages 12 (or the onset of puberty) to 18 years.* Adolescence is the time when people create their own unique *identity. Role confusion* is the alternative when the adolescent acquiesces to what society as a whole or someone in particular says he or she is to be. We need help from sources other than our parents in navigating this difficult and dangerous landscape. Teenagers join gangs, clubs, and teams because intuitively they know they need help to move into adulthood. They need older friends. They need rites of passage. There are a million ways to answer the question, "Who am I?" successfully. A person can be an intellectual or a mechanic or a bird watcher or an athlete or all of these. The primary way this question is answered incorrectly is when a teenager lets someone else answer on his or her behalf: "You are a lazy student"; "You will be a doctor"; "You are big breasted." If you succeed in moving through this life stage, you will achieve what Erikson calls "fidelity."

> "I require each of my students, during the semester, to turn in a credo, something that moves them from 'So and so said,' to 'I believe.'"
>
> —MOLLY MARSHALL

That means you have determined who you are on your own and are internally aware of your own identity ("I am Jewish"; "I am honest"; "I am a female"; "I am an optimist"). You now have the capacity to claim your distinctiveness. If you are confused about who you are, you may spend your life wavering and attempting to please the bully *de jour*.

6. *Young adult years, ages 19 to 40 years.* The challenge in this stage is *intimacy versus isolation*. Through adolescence, we were operating out of someone else's vision for us. Assuming we came to some resolution of our identity during adolescence, now we must go through the process of seeing if this unique "me" actually works out. If you decide you wanted to be a surgeon, do you have the aptitude, the study skills, the stomach for blood, and whatever else is required for that task? These are the years when a person is able to discover a thing or two about love. If you are able to forgive your significant other(s) for being fallible, to have grace for the people in your life in spite of their failures, then you can achieve some sort of intimacy. Some people, however, are never able to sustain intimacy because it is too painful. Someone in their young life has disappointed them (a lover, a boss, a mentor, a friend, a parent) and they isolate themselves from such heartache in the future. Intimacy requires two fallible *human* beings, not two perfect robots! People who cannot tolerate imperfection isolate themselves because there is not a marriage in the world, a work setting on the planet, or a friendship in the universe that does not require grace and forgiveness. This is the age at which the ideal meets the real, and there is the opportunity to learn the skill of adapting.

7. *Middle adult years, ages 40 to 65 years.* The conflict in this stage of maturity (and growth should still be happening!) is *generativity versus stagnation*. I know too many people who grew normally and appropriately through age 20 or 30, yet never learned another thing about themselves or life after that. While sexual creativity (having sex which in turn leads to having babies) can be a *selfish* act, it is at least one indication that generativity has occurred. At a later age, generativity must be a *selfless* act, an act of unreciprocated kindness. Grandparents write a book of stories for their grandchildren, never expecting anything in return. Some older citizens volunteer as docents at a museum or as helpers at the hospital for the sheer pleasure of doing something worthwhile for others. The opposite is stagnation, another example of the shutting down of all growth processes. I know people who, when they turn some arbitrary age such as 60, quit many of their volunteer activities. They resign from the choir. They no longer partic-

ipate in their professional sorority or fraternity. They pull back. They avoid new commitments. They even cease some of their long-term altruistic associations. They watch too much television. They play too much golf. While this is certainly a time to simplify and avoid overextension and stress, it is not a time to stop making a meaningful contribution.

8. *Maturity, ages 65 years to death.* Erikson contends that the work of this stage in life, beginning some time around retirement, has to do with *ego integrity versus despair.* The human body is no longer as useful for many of the things it accomplished in previous decades. Friends have died or are dying. Depression is understandable. Yet not all older people "go downhill" emotionally, even if they do deteriorate physically. My colleague, Horace Hammett, about age 75 at the time I was 25, told me, "You become what you've been becoming." Dr. Hammett was contending that, under ordinary circumstances, even as mental processes slow or weaken in old age, your personality continues in the direction you have trained it to go for the remainder of your natural life. If you have been a loving and kind person, then, even when you are not totally in control of your facilities, you remain a loving and kind person. On the other hand, if you were constantly angry and enraged in the privacy of your home (and your heart), and you hid your abusive nature from the public, then Dr. Hammett's theory is that when you age and have less control of your emotions, you will probably give evidence of the more contemptible character that once was hidden. If you were always fearful, but you hid your fear well, in old age your fear will be maximized, even to the point of paranoia. Approaching death without fear is Erikson's ideal, and it completes the circle. He writes, "Healthy children will not fear life if their elders have integrity enough not to fear death" (*Childhood and Society* [New York: Norton, 1950] 269).

> For everything there is a season,
>    And for every activity under heaven, there is a time:
> A time to be born,
>    And a time to die,
> A time to plant,
>    And a time to uproot,
> A time to kill,
>    And a time to heal,
> A time to break down,
>    And a time to build up,
> A time to weep,

And a time to laugh,
A time for mourning,
   And a time for dancing, . . .
A time to love,
   And a time to hate,
A time for war,
And a time for peace. (Ecclesiastes 3:1-4, 8)

# Chapter 9

# There Is No Fantasyland

Issue: *Knowledge*

> Objectives: I will be as informed as I can reasonably be. I will learn from my own experiences and from other people. I will be honest with myself. I will feel what I feel when I feel it. I will have hopes and dreams, but I will attempt to ground myself in reality.

Wisdom is far more than facts or knowledge. Wisdom includes appropriate, accurate, and proportionate truth tempered with compassion! But facts and knowledge are a good place to begin the pursuit of wisdom.

At one time in my life, I had certain beliefs:

1. Dogs were males and cats were females.
2. Pregnant women had eaten a watermelon seed, and the watermelon was growing inside them.
3. Santa Claus, the Easter Bunny, and the Tooth Fairy were real.
4. My mom and dad were better Christians than my pastor and his wife because my mom and dad only had two kids, which indicated they had had sex (whatever that meant) twice, and the pastor had four children which showed he and his wife had had sex four times.
5. Saying the word "pregnant" was wrong. If the "condition" required a word, "expecting" was preferred.
6. As a young entrepreneur, I thought I could sell two pieces of penny bubble gum for three cents. I learned I was wrong when I sat in front of our house on a busy street all day long and sold none.
7. All Russians were bad.
8. All Americans were good.
9. Black people were somehow inferior to white people.

10. I could trust people to do what they said they would do.

11. Having an "official" forum (radio, television, pulpit, or print media) suggested that a person must be right. People would say, "I heard it on the radio. It must be true."

12. North Augusta, South Carolina, was the capital of the world and its geographical center.

13. School teachers did not curse.

14. All families had a mother and a father.

15. Powerful and important people (especially those in the church, school, politics, and military) were good and right and were to be respected and obeyed.

16. People who drank alcohol were immoral and wicked.

17. Marriages should always be full of romance and continuously happy. If married people argued, something was wrong with the marriage.

18. My religious heritage provided the only right way to be in good standing with God.

19. Foreigners or immigrants who had difficulty with the English language were not as smart as "normal" people without accents. (It did not occur to me, until embarrassingly late in my life, that the person struggling with English was at least bilingual—many immigrants speak or understand three or four languages—and I was the dolt with limited linguistic skills.)

Knowledge is much more than power. It is money. It is weight loss. It is health. Information improves job performance. Relevant facts can improve relationships. Yet, rarely do schools teach a course called "General Knowledge for Living" or "Life 101" or "Essential Data for Getting Along in the World." Other than what you learn, almost by osmosis, from family and other significant people in your young life, you march toward adulthood unaware that information, skill sets, and tools exist that could improve every area of your life. Why do we take courses in world history and remain clueless about family history? Our school systems teach anthropology, the generic study of humankind, ten thousand times more often than courses that help us think about our intimate relationships.

In order to mature, we do need to think about what went on in our homes as we grew up. If we intentionally do not

> "I've learned that to ignore the facts does not change the facts."
>
> —ANDY ROONEY

reflect on our parents and family systems, we are most likely (a) to mimic them unconsciously or (b) to reject them rebelliously and mindlessly. A much wiser course is to sort through the habits of our families and culture and choose which ones we want to keep and which we want to leave behind.

## Knowledge

I have learned that there are two kinds of information, and each has its place. There is the hard data ($2 + 2 = 4$), and there are softer bits of information that are no less true (I like jazz and I enjoy baseball). Life is made up of both. Some people prefer the former and deny the dependability of the latter. They are suspicious of what might be called the subjective world, of anything connected to feelings and opinions. But someone once told me that "Feelings are facts," and I have never heard a good argument against that truth. If I don't like broccoli, then you can't make me like broccoli. You can't argue me into liking broccoli. Logic is not the issue.

I was on the board of a nonprofit organization that was unsurprisingly strapped for money. One of the resources of that organization was a quarterly newsletter that listed continuing education opportunities in the state. The circular was a low-budget document produced as a labor of love by a volunteer. I appreciated getting it and occasionally went to one of the events advertised. At one of our board meetings, the executive of the organization asked if the board members, representing the larger constituency, would be willing to pay to receive the newsletter. I said I would not. He began to argue with me about how it was worth a $5 subscription fee. I interrupted him to remind him of his question. I was not willing to pay for this service. It was a nice perk of membership in the organization and a desirable benefit, but on a subscription basis, there were other magazines and journals I would pay for first. Was he going to go around the state arguing with people one by one about the value of our occasional circular? He resisted hearing the truth, and the truth was that I did not value that document enough to pay five dollars for it.

Physical, emotional, and spiritual health requires both kinds of truth—the hard data and the softer evidence. One is not more valuable than the other. Statisticians (my younger daughter is one) and scientists do a magnificent job of getting us the best numbers available. But they are often put on the right course by paying attention to the scientifically unverified anecdotes that are part of everyday life, the "buzz" about what is going on, whether good, bad, or indifferent.

People who are maturing and growing are those who take notice of and pay heed to both kinds of information. Ignorance is not bliss! Ignorance is ignorance. To be ignorant is to be powerless and helpless. Ignorance means making unnecessary mistakes. Ignorance is costly. Ignorance is folly.

Good information is a powerful ingredient to help us move toward the lives we want for ourselves. Facts and truth are not optional. They are essential. Good decisions are easier to make when we have ample and accurate information. Sometimes data is easily available. If certain jobs appeal to us, we need to know the educational requirements or other prerequisites for those careers. Nobody stumbles into being an engineer or a judge or a welder. Certain academic courses must be taken. Facts must be learned. I remember a conversation with one young man, approaching thirty, who wanted to be a college baseball coach, but he had not even finished college.

Unrealistic attitudes and behavior (that is, what is not real or factual) can almost always go in two directions, making it tricky to get at the truth. A 200-pound woman decides at Thanksgiving that she wants to weigh 120 pounds by Christmas. This is not realistic. But the other extreme is the 200-pound woman who says she can't lose weight because she is "big-boned." This is also unrealistic. Both attitudes are a fantasy.

In every transition in my life from less desirable behavior to more desirable behavior, in moving from where I didn't want to be to where I wanted to be, facts have been an important tool. Weight Watchers is not casual about the weekly weigh-in. That is the moment of accountability. You don't lose much weight if you pay no attention to the scales and if you don't count calories.

Solutions to problems will inevitably involve different behaviors than the ones that got you in your current mess. If you are addicted to too much television, you have a couple of choices: turn the television off completely, or allow yourself a set number of hours each week. By definition, numbers are quantifiable. Then you have to tally. "I'm going to try to watch less TV" seldom works. Watch your favorite show for thirty minutes or one hour, or whatever you determine to allow yourself, and then turn off the TV. If your difficulty relates to finances, there is no substitute for a budget that takes into account your real income and anticipates your actual expenses, including paying off debt. Hoping you win the lottery is not a good strategy. Wishing life were better is not a healthy way of coping. You need facts. Whatever happens in the future is based on reality. I am an optimist, but vague wishful thinking will not alter anything in my life or your life. It won't improve my relationship with my parents, my children, or my spouse. The doctor who prescribes medication has not merely guessed about the correct dosage. He or she has invested immeasurable hours in learning hard data in order to prescribe the right medication. Too much creates one kind of problem, and too little creates another. Facts are good, and people who solve problems work with facts. The world is not organized so that we can do whatever we want and be exempt from the consequences. There is no Fantasyland, except at Disney World.

If information were easily accessible merely for the asking, everyone could get equally rich on the stock market or get a Ph.D. with little or no effort. Everyone would attain their dream job and woo their dream spouse. But precision and candor are rare commodities. People pay a lot of money and work hard to earn advanced degrees. Education involves professors telling you when you are wrong, not merely affirming your preexisting behaviors or opinions. If having legitimate and meticulous data is a requirement for achievement in any

> "Get the data."
>
> —ROBERT MCNAMARA,
> THE FOG OF WAR

endeavor, no wonder so few of us are successful. People do not want to do the work—and it is work—to discover the relevant facts, to ask the hard questions, to make themselves vulnerable to criticism, to move past their knee-jerk emotional responses, to evaluate the commonly accepted wisdom of the culture, and to make the changes required to achieve their goals.

Some individuals, admittedly, seem to be lucky for a while, but pure chance is chancy. Penang, Malaysia, is a picturesque island with an absurdly high death rate from motorcycle accidents. When I got off the plane there on my first trip to the Far East, determined not to be the American with strong opinions about the superiority of my way of life, I failed my first test miserably. In front of the airport, I saw a two-year-old boy standing on the back of a motorcycle, holding the adult driver's shoulders, as they took off down the street. What foolishness! On the island, motorcycles are a practical and cheap means of transportation. But the operation and handling of those tiny vehicles was breathtaking, often permanently, literally, and irreversibly so. I saw as many as five people on a single small motorcycle. In a "yield" situation where two vehicles were to merge into one lane, a motorcycle carrying two or three passengers would scoot between the two merging automobiles or trucks. Fortunately, they usually succeeded.

When I asked my hosts about this reckless driving, they confirmed what I already suspected. This was a society in which fate, luck, destiny, and fortune were hugely important: they believe that when it is your time to die, you die. There are people in every country and every religion who believe that. I heard an obese, undereducated Baptist preacher in South Carolina say the same thing once. But he is wrong and he is living dangerously. I like facts. I want to bend the odds for life, health, and success in my direction, and accurate information helps me do this.

In my effort to shed weight, I believe I can attribute twenty pounds of permanent lost pounds to gathering new information I did not have when I was at my peak weight. Losing those twenty pounds did not require character or discipline or moral fiber or courage. I just needed facts. (Losing weight past those twenty pounds did require character and discipline and moral fiber and courage!) Weight Watchers uses a point system in their program, and every food, from a wedge of lettuce to a T-bone steak, from marinara sauce to blueberries, is assigned a point value. On my first morning on the Weight Watchers program, I ate what I believed to be a healthy, low-calorie breakfast of a cup of granola, a cup of low-fat milk, a banana, and coffee with cream and an artificial sweetener. I counted my points and discovered I had eaten half my food allotment for the day! With better choices, including lighter cereals, skim milk, and an entire cup of berries, I can have a great breakfast for far fewer calories.

But a full stockpile of facts is not part of an inner bank of information we receive at birth. The ability to count calories is not encoded on our DNA. We are not born knowing how to fight fair or how to get out of credit card debt. Our parents may or may not teach us how to cook healthy foods or balance a checkbook. No parent can teach children everything they need to know about food, finances, relationships, and careers. Speaking as a parent, most of us do the best we can, instructing our children about safety, manners, and a host of other issues. We trust that schools will teach them world history, arithmetic, grammar, reading, and science. We hope they are socialized by taking dance lessons or playing on the soccer team. They learn some of our own family traditions: fishing, travel, theater, dancing, auto mechanics, carpentry, cooking, or sewing. They discover many things on their own, but most topics are left untaught. Occasionally, our children are taught incorrectly. After all, there is no Santa Claus, and most of us tell them there is. Maybe a ten-year-old should eat everything on her plate, but a fifty-year-old should probably not.

If you are deficient in information about a subject that is important to you, it is your responsibility to learn what you need to know in order to function as an adult in our society. You can blame your parents, but that is wasted energy. You can be mad at your spouse or your boss for not having told you everything you wish they had told you. Ultimately, though, no one is going to live your life for you. Find out what you need to know to function in our world. You will do better fully informed than ignorant.

Folly comes in many shapes and sizes, and accurate information is merely one step in a lifelong process of learning to get life "right." Young adults have not yet had sufficient life experience to make all the best choices possible. My list at the beginning of this chapter is an example. It takes time and opportunity to overcome inexperience and misinformation! There is too much data to be assimilated. Youth, according to Erik Erikson, is when teens sort through various options to discover their own identities. Skilled teachers, mentors, and coaches are invaluable during these formative years. However, even impressive models can be problems for at least two reasons: (1) your abilities and aptitudes may not be the same as your idol's and, (2) sooner or later, your hero will almost certainly expose weaknesses.

Of course, age does not automatically qualify one as wise. I heard a motivational speaker tell of a fifty-year-old man who missed a promotion. "Why did that thirty-year-old get the job?" the senior employee complained. "I've had twenty years of experience with the company, and she has only had five."

"No," his boss countered, "she has had five years of experience, but you have had only one year of experience twenty times."

Not every person profits or learns from the past. The biggest problem I see as people fail at job after job and relationship after relationship is that they continue to make the same mistakes. The best predictor of the future is the past because too many people fail to learn from their mistakes. If the guy you are dating has been to jail three times for drug possession, he is probably not the best choice for a secure, drug-free future. He can change, and you can change, but his history is a fact that is good to know! This is why prospective employers check references. We don't do that in relationships. We take a person's word that how they described the last break-up was actually the way it happened. We lack knowledge.

## *Nuance versus Naïveté*

All so-called "facts" are not true! Just because the person you meet on a blind date tells you his or her last partner was a jerk, you do not now know as an irrefutable fact that the former flame actually was a jerk. Maybe they were; maybe they weren't. It is too early to be certain. What is the objective evidence for that opinion? Your date will tell you one side of the saga, but empathy—the effort and ability to perceive what someone else feels and experiences—is necessary for competent decision-making. If the former partner were telling you his or her version, what would you hear? There is always more to the story than you know.

We all need critical filters through which to sift the sights, sounds, and words that bombard us daily. Being rich or famous or powerful does not automatically make one wise. Just because the general informs the president that this is a worthy war does not mean it is a worthy war. Just because a magazine article tells you this is a reprehensible war does not mean it is a reprehensible war. At some point, an adult should learn to assess and evaluate data. Just because the preacher said it does not mean it is true. Just because a lawyer said something does not make it correct. You can find an attorney who will take a different position. How do *you* come to a decision? Do you believe the person who seems to be the most religious? Do you believe the person who is most charming? Do you believe the person who has the most money or prestige or who is prettiest or most powerful? Do you trust only Democrats and never Republicans, or vice versa? Is a deodorant or automobile truly superior just because a movie star or ball player advertises it?

> "The problem is that when we are low on facts, and when important issues stay underground, we are high on fantasy and emotionality—anger included."
>
> —HARRIET G. LERNER,
> *THE DANCE OF ANGER*

How trustworthy is a particular source? What is their motivation? Money? Votes? Power? I believe every person has the capacity to be self-serving. If I am trying to get a job with your firm, I will put my best foot forward. I am not going to confess all my deficiencies up front. If you are trying to hire me, you will tell me your company's finest attributes, not its least attractive. Naïveté or innocence can be enchanting. It can also be deadly.

People allow themselves to become casualties of naïveté in several ways.

*1. Exaggeration and understatement*—Some inaccuracy is the consequence of personality. The "drama queen" who wants attention exaggerates her situation: "It's the hottest day ever." The proclamation will not stand up to scrutiny. The hottest day "ever" turns out to be a warm spring afternoon. It will get much hotter later in the summer, and she will gladly sit in her bikini at the beach without a word of complaint. Any parent or teacher knows this drill. Petty complaints are a standard part of the world of children: "Mom, tell her to stop looking at me."

As people grow older, it is appropriate that they learn to respond minimally or not at all to unimportant issues. Certain words are often a clue to unbalanced and disproportionate responses: appalled, awful, disgusting, outrageous, ridiculous, shocked, stupid, unforgivable, ruined.

Read the "Letters to the Editor" section of your local newspaper, and you will see more of those words in one day than are necessary for a lifetime. Is it truly shocking and unforgivable, not to mention outrageous and ridiculous, that a city council member voted to spend money or not to spend money in a way with which you disagree? Politicians make decisions every day that I find perplexing. I am going to save the word "appalled" for more serious crimes.

Making a mountain out of a molehill is one way to be mistaken, and another equally erroneous way is to make a molehill out of a mountain. The goal is to get it right, to have truthful and accurate information. I have attended funerals for stubborn men who ignored a pain or a rash (that grew until it killed them) because it seemed too small a thing with which to be bothered.

*2. Knee-jerk traditionalist/conformist*—Our parents and teachers taught us the simplest lessons possible when we were children. After all, they did not have time to reason with us prior to every potential danger. "Do not go near the road" was a universal admonition for a three-year-old child, but it would not be appropriate or adequate for a pre-adolescent, and it certainly doesn't make sense for a college student. We are supposed to adjust as we grow. Blind obedience to a childhood reprimand or family tradition makes no sense when we are forty. A parent's goal is to make a young child without good judgment less adventurous. That should not be a parent's goal as the child gets older. Unfortunately, sometimes parents still enjoy having their children under their control, even when they are adults.

On a more humorous note, I heard about a man who went to his physician after a fall in his garden. "Nothing more than a bad bruise," said his doctor. She then told him to put heat on his bruise and it would be better in a few days.

"Heat?" he asked. "My mom told me to put cold compresses on a bruise."

"I'm the doctor," she replied, "and my mother told me to put heat on bruises."

Breaking old habits, beliefs, and traditions is almost always challenging.

3. *Black-and-white thinking*—All-or-nothing thinking can create unnecessary turmoil. The best person, the top company, the preeminent school, the finest church, the dominant country, the finest family—each has negative components. None is perfect. Conversely, no one is so bad that there is no glimmer of truth, hope, or charity in his or her life. Great literature exposes the complexity of human nature. There are tragic and fatal flaws even in admirable individuals. Biographers often startle the public with unanticipated revelations about a popular person's hidden flaws.

The inability to grant nuances to reality is a form of ignorance. Many Evangelical Christians, fundamentalist Muslims, secular humanists, and people of various other stripes are unable to discern the good outside their own faith or intellectual system: "All Jews are going to hell." "All Republicans are crooks." "Anyone who attended the university of (fill in the name of your school's rival) is an idiot." "You can't trust white people."

I have discovered that certain "universal" words are clues to thinking that is likely to be wrong: all, always, best, completely, every, everybody, never, nobody, none, nothing, number one, perfect, unsurpassable, worst.

When you use these words, and especially when you overuse them, you move toward inaccuracy. Even if you are correct in some of your opinions, you lose credibility if you make pronouncements that are patently wrong: "My school is better than your school in every sport. And all of our students are smarter, too." We might expect a sixteen-year-old cheerleader to make such claims, but a middle-aged grownup should be more careful. Fanatics (fans) can be laughable when all they are defending is their school's football team, but there is nothing humorous about extremism in politics, religion, and other important areas of life. When people abdicate their right to think for themselves and give power to charismatic individuals who seem to make life simple and clear, then society is in trouble. That happened in Nazi Germany. It happened in Communist Russia. It may happen someday in a mentally lazy and economically greedy United States of America. Neither the Republican nor the Democrats, neither the Protestants nor the Catholics, neither black nor white, neither male nor female have all the truth. We had better listen to and learn from each other if we are to survive and thrive.

A few years ago, I attended my five-year-old grandson's soccer game. One of the children kicked the ball, which careened at a right angle to the goal. The coach said, encouragingly, "Good kick."

Actually, it was a horrible kick. At some point, for that child to improve, some coach or parent is going to have to call a bad kick a bad kick. That is when the child will have the opportunity to grow and improve. Encouragement is more important than accuracy at age five, so the coach said the right thing, but when mature adults still think a bad kick is the same as a good kick, they will encounter unnecessary problems. Doing what comes naturally is ordinarily a recipe for failure. Healthy marriages, fit bodies, satisfying jobs, and successes in any other endeavor require information and effort. As long as we think bad kicks are okay, and no one instructs us differently, we will be mired in mediocrity and futility.

> "What gets us into trouble is not what we don't know. It's what we know for sure that just ain't so."
>
> —MARK TWAIN

## Stubbornness

I have a friend about whom it is often said, "He may be wrong, but he is never in doubt." Stubbornness is a form of mental and emotional laziness. Such people already have their minds made up, don't want to think about something, or, famously, will "think about it tomorrow." I am fascinated by the number of conservative college students who sign up for a required philosophy or religion course at their liberal arts college and are determined not to be affected (translation: not to learn anything) by "liberal" professors before they even hear a word uttered in a classroom.

Sometimes the professor could be wrong. But sometimes my parents or my childhood beliefs could be wrong, or my favorite tenth grade teacher could be wrong. My former colleague Terry Brooks believes a person cannot truly mature until he or she is able to acknowledge the limitations and mistakes of childhood role models, until he or she comes to terms with the imperfection of seminal teachers and influences. Terry is right. That is why growing up is so painful to the child and the parent! What made sense when I was fifteen years old does not necessarily make sense for me as an adult who is trying to work his way through totally different life circumstances.

One of my family scripts was, "Don't study too hard." My dad, a brilliant man who never had much ambition, was affected as a high school student by a class valedictorian's suicide. I heard that story many times. So my brother and I were encouraged to be "well-rounded," which is excellent advice for anybody. But that translated into my underachievement. I could get by in high school and, though I hate to admit it, in college, with little or no study. I was a B and C student. I eventually went to grad school and discovered I had a brain. I earned a Master's degree and a Doctorate. The old study habits (which I didn't have) had to change.

One of the saddest attacks of negative nostalgia I have encountered was while reading Frank McCourt's second autobiographical book *'Tis* (New York: Scribners, 2000). His first installment, *Angela's Ashes*, was a bestselling account of the grinding poverty of his childhood. I could not identify with it. He was more impoverished than anybody I knew. However, *'Tis*, which described his early years as an Irish immigrant in America, struck home. His account of moving up the educational and socioeconomic ladder recalled, for me, a couple of episodes in my own life. A family member or a work buddy in a dead-end job challenged McCourt's attempt to get an education, to use good grammar, and to play by a different set of rules than was valued on the lowest rungs of society. I identified with that; I had heard it all: "Do you really think you are better than us now?" "You are getting kind of uppity, aren't you?"

There was and is a mammoth conspiracy afoot by the ignorant to keep others as wretched as they are! Misery, we say, loves company. It makes underachievers feel better if you are failing along with them. However, you can improve yourself if you will. It is not necessary that the poverty or misery of your childhood and youth be the reality of your maturity.

## Walking the Middle Ground

On another front, my parents, who were decent and moral people, were also products of their culture and their parents' culture, and that means they were racists. Every fiber of my being, including even the Bible they read to me, and the songs they sung to me ("red and yellow, black and white, they are precious in his sight; Jesus loves the little children of the world") required that I reject the racism of my parents and my childhood church. Growing up and beyond your childhood beliefs is a painful process.

Culture, schools, religion, and parents have both conserving and liberating dimensions. Both are necessary. Anyone who only knows how to protect traditions, who always resists change, who is addicted to the past, is already spiritually and emotionally dead. Anyone who is only interested in challenging the status quo, whose motto is "Change for change's sake," is a loose cannon and potentially dangerous.

The challenge of the maturing person is to walk in that middle (moderate!) ground, which will probably make both the traditionalist and the revolutionary unhappy. The person who is serious about his or her emotional and spiritual maturity must decide which traditions are permanent and which are transient. "Don't steal" is a keeper. "Women shouldn't wear pants" is not.

People fear knowledge because it is revealing. People see things about themselves they don't want to see, and they certainly don't want other people to see these deficiencies. But growth and maturity will not come until a person is willing to "face the facts."

# Chapter 10

# Out of Control

*Isssue: Addiction*

Objectives: I will mind my own business, make first things first, live and let live, "fake it 'til I make it," and remember that recovery is work.

Addiction deserves extra attention. While there are "popular" and obvious addictions to alcohol, cigarettes, coffee, drugs, eating, credit card debt, and sex, other individuals fall victim to hundreds of less obvious obsessions and compulsions. You can become addicted to almost anything, from coupon-clipping to nail-biting to television-watching to text-messaging to fishing to Internet blogs. The clue is whether your activity has an "off" switch, whether you can walk away from it if something more important comes along—for example, a weekend with family or friends. Can you stop the activity whenever it becomes a problem? Can you moderate it?

One of the problems with addictions is that, by definition, nothing else is "more important." We lose control. Whether the preoccupation is with religion, politics, work, or food, we rationalize our addictive activity with justifications that sound grand: "My golf is what lets me maintain my mental health." "If you think I'm a basket case now, you should see me when I'm not smoking." "My work is what puts food on the table. Don't ask me to slow down." "I must go to the church every Thursday night. After all, I am chair of the Flower Committee." "How do people live who do not keep their houses neat? I couldn't exist in that kind of chaos."

You may need someone else to help you discover if you have addictions and what they are. Many of us do. Or you may know exactly what your compulsions are because the evidence has surrounded you for a long time.

For the purposes of this chapter, I return to my confession that I talk too much. I also eat too much. I am addicted to coffee and caffeine in the morning, and if I don't drink some, I get a headache. But constant chatter and the corollary of not listening well are the best examples of my big compulsions. A predilection to verbosity probably isn't your problem, but it will allow me to illustrate one area where my life was out of control. You will have to be honest about your own cravings, urges, and obsessions.

In a Dick Francis novel titled *Banker* (New York: Putnam, 1983), the narrator

> "It's like getting rid of an alley cat. You don't have to kick it; just don't feed it."
>
> —GERALD MAY, *ADDICTION AND GRACE*

introduces a character with these words: "Alec, my own age, suffered, professionally speaking, from an uncontrollable bent for frivolity. It brightened up the office no end, but as court jesters seldom made it to the throne, his career path was observably sideways and erratic." That could have been written about me anytime between high school and age forty. The key word is "uncontrollable." I could not be restrained. When it came to my need to talk, to entertain, to keep other people happy, I had no self-regulation, no "off" button. I inherited this propensity for mindless chatter honestly. The Aldridges will talk to a fencepost. The Aldridges gravitate toward jobs in sales. It is no accident that my first career was as a Baptist preacher. Think about it: hundreds of people sat quietly while I talked. I hoped they would listen, but it almost didn't matter to me as long as I could talk. My problem wasn't that what I said was full of errors or mean-spirited. It was that I said too much!

Talking was a huge part of my life, not just in my family, but also in my culture. Southerners are supposed to be hospitable, accommodating, friendly, gregarious, gracious, and charming. The list of words can go on forever, but most of them meant, at least to me, that I was invited and even expected to take the lead socially, to put people at ease, to make them feel accepted and comfortable.

Did you catch that? I am supposed to help *them* feel comfortable, even if it means ignoring my own feelings of discomfort. It is the nature of family scripts that they trump most everything else: wisdom, justice, and compassion. We do what comes naturally (at least what seems natural to us), no matter how stupid our behavior is, no matter how wrong it may seem to the rest of the world, no matter how counter-productive our actions are.

We all have self-justifications for addictive behavior: "My family eats too much." "Everybody drinks when they join the Army." "When I started using, the drugs were free and made me feel good."

Someone else growing up in my Southern culture may have learned to be demure, modest, attentive, and socially cautious. But there was only one option with regard to my Southern Baptist evangelical church culture. We were to go and tell, to preach, to proclaim, to teach, to evangelize. Have you ever seen a quiet evangelist? That would be an oxymoron. Have you ever known a Baptist monk who has taken a vow of silence? Of course not. My culture, my church, and my family not only gave me permission to talk, they *expected* me to talk. They demanded it. I was not a good Christian, according to my tradition, if I was not attempting to persuade you to join our club.

(Let me note here that Southern Baptist evangelists have their share of problems, but so does everyone else. I know people who talk too much who fit in other categories. Is any group exempt? I also know people who talk too little, who do not speak up when a good word is needed. This is my story, so I point out my addiction and the foibles of my traditions. I have been exorcising my own demons for thirty years—with some success! I hope you understand the illustrative nature of my story so you can begin the process of understanding your own peculiar issues.)

I grew up talking.

All the sordid details of my need to talk would bore you, but this was an obvious problem I needed to resolve, and the only way for that to happen was for *me* to change. I needed to shut up. This was the single most difficult assignment I undertook in my attempt to write new life scripts. My need to jabber manifested itself in embarrassing ways. When I was twenty-five years old, I remember being on a fifteen-minute car trip with my boss during which I must have talked for fourteen minutes. I was completely out of control.

Family scripts have a way of rearing their heads in uneven and uncomfortable social situations. When I was fearful of losing prestige or standing, when I believed it was in my best interest, when I thought it was my task to impress someone, then I fell back on deep-rooted, ill-considered habits, even if those habits actually drove people away or made them think less of me. When I was in a relationship with a social equal, my need to dominate conversation was reduced, but it still didn't go away. When I was in what I intuitively believed was a socially superior position, I was more aware of my need to listen. I was less compelled to meet my own needs, and I was willing to work to meet someone else's.

I began to confront my addiction by setting modest goals. For example, if my wife and I went to a college football game (two hours away) with another couple, then simple arithmetic and courtesy would suggest that I talk for no more than one-fourth of the trip. If I were having a three-way conversation with two buddies at a coffee shop, then my goal would be to allow myself no more than one-third of the floor time. If there were eight people in a supper club, then I intended to speak a maximum of one-eighth of the time we were together. I am embarrassed to admit this, but the truth compels me to confess that it was more than a year before I achieved my goal even a single time. I was out of control.

> "I still have bad days, but that's okay because I used to have bad years."
>
> —ANONYMOUS

Once, I was in a conference that was to last several days. About twenty people were involved. Most of us did not know each other, and the group leader decided we should spend the first session becoming acquainted. Rather than simply going around the circle, we were asked to introduce ourselves randomly. In such circumstances in the past, I would have been one of the first to take my turn. In high school and college, I was always first. I was so utterly clueless that it never occurred to me to do anything other than what bubbled up naturally. To my credit, as I matured into young adulthood, I learned to resist the need to be first and to wait until several other people had taken their turn. On this particular occasion, I set the specific goal for myself of being the last person. Somebody had to be last, and I was trying to write a new life script. The process took more than an hour. I sat smugly for the first half-dozen or so introductions. I thought this self-discipline would be easy. The first half-dozen people made their introductions in a timely fashion, and I was pleased with how my small exercise at self-improvement was going.

Then the pain began. Apparently, some people are as out of control in their need not to speak as I have always been in my need to break the silence. The process slowed to a crawl. There were long pauses as the last several participants seemed reticent to speak. Meanwhile, I was quiet. Part of the discipline I had set for myself on this occasion was utter silence until the last person, other than me, had introduced herself or himself. I was not going to use humor to diffuse the situation. I was not going to explain my silence by announcing that I intended to go last. I was going to say nothing until it was my turn. I was simply going to be last. There was tension in the room. At least I thought so. As the last few refused to speak up, I was thinking, "Are you people dumb? Are you stupid? Do you not understand the rules?

Everyone has got to do this. Say something." The silences were interminable. They seemed like hours to me. I sat quietly. Three people were left. Finally, one went. We were down to two. We sat. No one said anything. Tense silence. People looked around the room. I said nothing. Finally, the other fellow said his piece. When he was through, I almost exploded with my now anticlimactic introduction.

This exercise in self-discipline was a momentous breakthrough for me. I was like an alcoholic who had stayed sober for one night. I wasn't sure what the future held, but this one effort to challenge my addiction was a success.

"Twelve-step" groups are so named because their members understand that overcoming an addiction is a demanding undertaking. Addicts can be in the process of recovering, but one step, one insight, or one action does not mean the addiction has been conquered. Since there are many types of twelve-step groups—helping people overcome addictions to alcohol, gluttony, drugs, and sex, among other things—here is a generic version that should be helpful whether your addiction is talking too much or collecting cats:

1. We admitted that we were powerless over our addiction—that our lives had become unmanageable.

2. We came to believe that a Power greater than ourselves could restore us to sanity.

3. We made a decision to turn our will and our lives over to the care of God as we understood God.

4. We made a searching and fearless moral inventory of ourselves, our strengths and weaknesses.

5. We admitted to ourselves, to God, and to another human being the exact nature of our wrongs.

6. We were entirely ready to have God remove these defects of character.

7. We humbly asked God to remove our shortcomings.

8. We made a list of all persons we had harmed, and became willing to make amends to them all.

9. We made direct amends to such people wherever possible, except when to do so would injure them or others.

10. We continued to take personal inventory, and when we were wrong we promptly admitted it.

11. We sought through prayer and meditation to improve our conscious contact with God, as we understood God, praying only for knowledge of God's will for us, and the power to carry that out.

12. Having had a spiritual awakening as the result of these steps, we tried to carry this message to others, and to practice these principles in all our affairs.

Many who read this list will assume it is irrelevant to them because they are not alcoholics, but this list deserves attention from gossips, debtors, and compulsive fanatics of every stripe. If you are unwilling or unable to say to yourself and to other appropriate people, "I fail miserably at . . . ," then you have not yet moved toward a resolution of your addiction or compulsion. Addictions are accompanied by an abundance of other unattractive traits: stubbornness, defensiveness, aggressiveness, carelessness, foolishness. Nobody wants to admit he or she has a problem. Why should you be different? But you will not begin to improve, to grow, until you admit, without equivocation, "I have a problem."

There are also twelve traditions in Alcoholics Anonymous and other twelve-step groups, but neither the sayings of AA found in its "Big Book" nor this volume can substitute for ongoing human relationships, guidance, mentoring, confession, sponsorship, accountability, and encouragement. The problems of addiction must be worked out in real life, and we all need

> "If you find yourself in a hole, the first thing to do is to stop digging."
>
> —ANONYMOUS

someone or some group to walk with us through the challenging circumstances we encounter. In addiction recovery, there is no substitute for accountability. I hesitate to say an addiction is impossible to overcome alone, but if you keep failing, then you need someone to hold you accountable. You need someone to walk with you through your time of healing. If a twelve-step group is not available, ask a friend or a therapist to meet with you periodically for counsel.

Listed below are a few of the lessons I learned when attending twelve-step groups:

Mind your own business.
First things first.
Live and let live.
Fake it 'til you make it.
I have authority over no life but my own.

Detach.

I don't have to go to every fight I'm invited to.

Doing what your heart says is the same as doing what your "script" says.

We always have choices.

I cannot hurt others without hurting myself.

Happiness is liking the people I meet, not meeting the people I like.

Act rather than react.

The only thing that is the end of the world is the end of the world.

Feelings are facts.

Stay away from "pity parties," your own or someone else's.

Let go and let God.

You need to set boundaries.

Recovery is work.

One day at a time. (There is no other valid approach to overcoming addictions. Sometimes it is one hour at a time, or one meal at a time, or one person at a time, or one act at a time.)

This too will pass. (Even when you think your urge or your compulsion is absolutely irresistible, get through the next fifteen minutes, then the next fifteen, one minute at a time if necessary.)

Addicts are "adrenaline junkies." If life is going well, they will often create an unnecessary crisis in order to act out their addictions. Addictions are self-centered and self-consuming. The world narrows down to this moment, this act. The addicted person thinks there is no other choice.

*Antwone Fisher* is a movie about a brilliant young naval officer with anger management problems (Fox Searchlight

> "There is a very fine line between 'hobby' and 'mental illness.'"
>
> —DAVE BARRY

Pictures, 2003). The protagonist saw no other option for responding to a crisis than to lose his temper. His constant theme was, "That's not my problem." Unfortunately, people will hurt you and disappoint you and anger you. That is nonnegotiable. The only person Antwone Fisher could change was Antwone Fisher. He finally admitted that he had some responsibility. Only then did his life change for the better. Confessing one's limitations does not come naturally, but it can transform a life.

In my addiction to talking, I acted as if I were the only person in a room to have a wise or funny response to whatever was said. I was always prepared with two or more short anecdotes that, in turn, set up a lengthier narrative. I still talk a lot, but now I am more in control. My life and my conversation are more manageable. If I am with a shy person, I will probably have more to say than they do, but maybe not. (By the way, when finally I was able to contain my unbridled tongue, people predictably asked if something was wrong with me. Was I ill? Was I mad at somebody? Were my feelings hurt? Why was I being so quiet?)

In a paradoxical twist to my addiction, one of the underlying needs of my constant conversation was the need to be liked. I have discovered that fewer words are more highly valued than too many. In reviewing a journal I kept at that time, I found this note I made shortly after my fortieth birthday (more than twenty years ago): "Reflecting on the positive experience of turning forty, I suspect that the taming of my tongue—as much as any other single factor—is involved in the improved opinion of others toward me." Other things were certainly going on in my life, but maintaining greater control over the words that came out of my mouth was a great help in my improved self-esteem and in the good will of others.

Addictions are tougher to change than mere habits. Like most other Americans, I am sure I watch too much TV. But when I give up television for any reason, the change requires little effort and is not painful. For me, watching TV is a habit, not an addiction. The twelve-step programs of groups such as Alcoholics Anonymous, Narcotics Anonymous, and Overeaters Anonymous require that you begin by admitting that you are powerless over an addiction *and* that your life has become unmanageable.

I want to emphasize the second portion of that declaration. If all is well, then you have no need to change. If all is not well, then you need to change. If the change is easy, then good for you. Maybe you are dealing with something that is merely a bad habit. If the change is not easy, then admitting the problem is the first step.

We are not all cursed by the same problem! Some people talk too much. Some people are compulsively quiet. Some people eat

> "What keeps happening, over and over? What do I keep doing, over and over? What do other people keep doing to me, over and over? Why do I need this to happen? How and why do I attract it?"
>
> —MELODY BEATTIE,
> *BEYOND CODEPENDENCY*

too much. Some eat too little. Some are addicted to approval. Some go out of their way to be a clown. Some are addicted to text messaging. Some individuals have moved from what once was a hobby they enjoyed to being engaged in a compulsion that controls them. You can be addicted to collecting baseball cards or using a credit card. Groupies follow rock musicians all over the world. One of the challenges of a book or a lecture is that if 1,000 people read or hear the words, there are 1,000 different demons that need to be addressed. One person is verbally abusive, another is obsessively tidy, and another is addicted to pornography. My addiction to words is only illustrative of the many ways people are out of control of their lives.

Here are two step-by-step lists that have helped me understand my addictions. The first is a sequence that many people go through, more or less in this order:

1. I am clueless that a problem exists.
2. I know there is a problem, but I do nothing about it.
3. I might hope some sort of magic will take the problem away.
4. I choose to do nothing about the problem.
5. I might acknowledge (to myself and/or to someone else) that I might need to do something about my problem.
6. I want to do something about my problem.
7. I intend/propose/plan to do something about my problem.
8. I get help/insight/clarification/encouragement from the Internet or from one or more human beings about my problem.
9. I will do something/take some action (no matter how small) about my problem. I am competent and capable.
10. I am doing something about my problem.
11. I did something about my problem.
12. I will check in with somebody about the progress I am making with my problem and will be accountable, either for positive reinforcement or for critical feedback.
13. I will celebrate my successes in dealing with my problem.
14. I will keep on doing something about my problem.

Thus, I move from

• hopeless denial to
• frustrated awareness to

- naïve blaming to
- tentative acknowledgment to
- hopeful preparation to
- attentive evaluation to
- determined action to
- satisfied serenity to
- conscious accountability to
- continuing contentment.

I am eventually transformed. I become a different person.

# Chapter 11

# Looking for Grace in All the Wrong Places

Issue: Kindness

> Objectives: I will accept my humanity and imperfections. I will acknowledge the universality of human failure, including my own, and therefore I will be less defensive and more gracious. I will learn how to live with love, joy, and peace.

According to Clyde Francisco, one of my graduate school professors, "Love is an old and tired word, having been forced to bear too much weight and to carry too heavy a burden." Writers, romantics, preachers, movie stars, and others throw around the word "love" as if everybody who uses it means the same thing. Yet teenagers say "I love you" in the back seat of a car to someone they didn't even know two hours earlier. Society blesses their definition by saying they have "made love." Another adolescent picks up a two-dollar trinket at the mall, shows it to her friend, and exclaims, "I just love this." An abusive father, full of alcoholic rage, shrieks to his preschool son as he is beating him, "I am doing this because I love you." Husbands and wives declare their love to one another and then misbehave.

Over the years, I've learned that love is not what you feel when someone makes you feel good, but what you do when someone makes you feel bad.

The Greeks had at least three words for love: *phileo*, indicating "brotherly love"; *eros*, signifying "sexual love," from which our word "erotic" is derived; and *agape*, meaning "perfect love," the word used in the Bible to describe God's love for us. The English language has dozens of words that might occasionally describe what we mean when we say, "love," from "I'd love to have a toothpick right now" to "Don't you just love her haircut?" to "I love my new dentist" to "He loves his football team." Who knows what anybody means by "love" anymore? That one word encompasses many definitions: adoration, affection, attraction, care for, charity, charmed by, compassion, concern for, delighted in/delighted by, desire, devotion, enamored, fondness, friendly, have a crush on, infatuation, interested in, like, long for, lust, obsessed, passionate about, puppy love, reverence, romance, smitten.

Some of these are still meaningful words, but others are weak. I have grown fond of certain expressive terms that still have power, charm, charisma, sparkle, and substance that address the issue of loving behavior: kindness, grace, empathy, and generosity. The subjects of kindness, grace, and love are too large for one chapter of one book, so I shall identify three of the obstacles we face in our attempts to engage in loving relationships, either as a person practicing loving kindness or as a recipient of affection.

> "A man has a little strength, a little hope, a little love. Those things are like seeds that are planted in all men. But if he keeps them to himself, they will wither away and die very quickly, and then God help that poor man because he will have nothing and life will not be worth living."
>
> —HOWARD FAST, *SPARTACUS*

## Love as Action versus Love as Emotion

Anybody ought to be able to be nice to another human being who says and does kind things on his or her behalf. What is not to like about someone who nourishes me with food, shelter, comfort, security, and hope? What is not to value and commend about someone who makes me feel safe? The problem comes when I am cast off, rejected, for whatever reason. What do I do then? Do I strike the offending party? Do I move on to the next contributor to my comfort? Or do I figure out what has changed in me or in my caregiver and discover if she or he needs my care for a while? Love is not what teenagers or young adults feel when they are discovering wonderful and charming things about a new person. Love is what mature adults (and even teenagers sometimes) *do* when the person with whom they have a covenant of mutual care and fidelity is unable or unwilling to continue as a contributing participant in the relationship. Thus, the wedding vows say, "for better or worse, for richer or poorer, in sickness and health, till death us do part." The question is not that you will love another person at the beginning of a relationship, when it is easy to be caring and compassionate. The question is how you will love one another later in that relationship when the going gets tough—when dementia or cancer set in, or when your beloved is simply having a bad day (or a bad year). The wedding vows attempt to answer that question: for better or worse.

Some people think they are "loving" when they are in fact being churlish, selfish, or cruel. Since every major religion in the world posits some variation of the golden rule, that seems a noble place to start: "Ask yourself what you want people to do for you, then grab the initiative and do it for them" (Jesus, Matthew 7, paraphrased in Eugene Peterson's *The Message*). The golden rule is the embodiment of "empathy." Unfortunately, we often balk at putting ourselves in the other person's shoes. Loving someone is work! We cannot imagine, without considerable effort, what they might want. If they don't want exactly what we want, then we have a problem.

Our life experience is never wide enough or deep enough to imagine every possible scenario, to know what a loving response would be from another's point of view. A corollary of the golden rule is to ask the people we attempt to love exactly what they believe they need from us. Probably the most loving thing we can do for someone is to listen. A few years ago, my employer got it right when we asked Bill and Evelyn to be our representatives among the poor in North Charleston. We told them to listen for a year. Instead of coming in with all the knowledge, answers, and resources, we told Bill and Evelyn to eavesdrop on the people in the Chicora/Cherokee community for an entire year. They did, and the result has begun to transform the community. They listened first, and spoke and acted later. Eugene Peterson, in his paraphrase of the Epistle of James, says we are to "Lead with our ears." What great advice!

When I was a young pastor at the First Baptist Church of Batesburg, South Carolina, like other churches in the region, ours promoted an annual "revival meeting" in which a preacher exhorted, challenged, inspired, and sermonized every night for a week. One year, instead of the usual revival word-fest, we sponsored a church and community seminar. We created a task force to listen to the community. Rather than continuing to barrel ahead with our own agendas, we asked what their needs were. The task force decided we needed to do something about drug and alcohol abuse in our small community, so we sponsored an event to begin that process. Resulting directly from that initiative was the creation of the first Alcoholics Anonymous group in the community. We offered the use of our church fellowship hall. That AA group recently celebrated its twenty-fifth anniversary! Which do you suppose did more good: an annual "revival" meeting full of talk, or an event in which we actually paid attention to and responded to the needs of the community?

Husbands need to listen to wives. Wives need to listen to husbands. Employees need to listen to bosses. Bosses need to listen to employees. Children need to listen to parents. Parents need to listen to children.

Long ago, when I was still single, a divorced female friend told me the sad story of her failed marriage. She described one Valentine's Day when she cooked her unappreciative husband an omelet in the shape of a heart. She thought this was a romantic gesture and that her ex-husband had been a jerk not to value her gift. Years later, as I reflected on her story, I wondered if she had met her need or his. Maybe the way to that husband's heart required the gift of a couple of fishing lures or some golf balls, not an omelet in the shape of a heart.

Are we listening to the person we attempt to love, or are we barreling ahead with our own agenda, meeting our needs rather than his or hers?

## Abstract versus Concrete

Another reason "love" is difficult to define is that devotion often plays out counter-intuitively. The kind-hearted prostitute turns out to be more generous, more compassionate, more charitable, and more full of grace than the local priest or rabbi who is mean, malicious, vengeful, unforgiving, generally unpleasant, and a lecher. How does that happen?

Let's begin with a confession that we don't know what we don't know. Everybody has a story, the virtuous and the vile, and those stories explain much that is otherwise inexplicable. If we knew all the "facts," we might better understand the prostitute's kindness and the priest's meanness. Being raised poor and poorly does not justify murder and misbehavior, as some social workers and attorneys might have us believe, but families and scripts do affect behavior for good and for ill. In *Mere Christianity* (San Francisco: HarperSanFrancisco, 2001), C. S. Lewis has an insightful essay titled "Nice People or New Men?" He argues that Citizen A, a religious person, is not as nice as Citizen B, an irreligious person. He contends that since Citizen A started off so deep in the hole with regard to being "nice," it is likely he or she will never catch up to Citizen B, who simply was blessed from birth onward with having a pleasing disposition, someone who, by temperament, has almost always been easy to get along with.

Still, even with that caveat, it is clear that many people of all faiths are unloving and unlovable jerks, and many people with little or no religious faith or ethics are easier to be around. Some people bring pleasure by entering the room, and some bring pleasure by leaving the room. We need to be careful and not confuse concepts such as "easier to be around," "people pleasers," and even "sweet and nice" as being descriptors of loving behavior. A parent who makes a misbehaving three-year-old unhappy may be loving. A boss who fires an incompetent employee may be doing the employee the biggest favor imaginable. A coach who disciplines a team member for inappropriate or lazy behavior may be more loving than the easygoing coach who doesn't care whether his players live or die, succeed or fail. As the administrator of a large organization, I am aware that everybody doesn't like me all the time. For a thousand reasons, I have made people mad. I have fired people, challenged people, and made people uncomfortable.

Loving someone else does not happen in the abstract. I am reminded of an old joke about a man watching kids from the fifth floor window of an office building. As he sees the children putting their handprints on and writing their names in the fresh concrete he has just paid to have poured, he mutters, "I have always preferred kids more in the abstract than in the concrete."

The problem with concepts such as "sweet and nice" is that they are abstract. They tell about your personality, but they say nothing about what you would do in a predicament. If someone I care for is being mugged, I

> "Love the Lord your God with all your heart, and with all your soul and with all your mind. The second commandment is like the first, Love your neighbor as you love yourself. All the Law and all the Prophets hang on these two commandments."
>
> —JESUS, MATTHEW 22:37-40

want a police officer who is not sweet and nice but who is courageous and willing to cause harm to the assailant, if necessary, in order to save my beloved. I believe that, in some way, that officer is also saving the assailant. Life is not lived out in theory. Ethical and loving behavior is often more an art than a science, which is why legalists get it wrong so often.

The trouble with "legalism," or merely following a set of rules, is that such systems require or prescribe a particular behavior in every instance, and allow for no nuance or shading. Thus, a mean (in the old sense of that word, "miserly") man counts pennies accurately, but misses the larger picture. Such people lack perspective. The arithmetic may come out right, but imprudent and damaging decisions are made in the process. Loving, kind, gracious behavior at least asks the question, "Which is more important: getting the details exactly right or paying attention to the human beings affected by these decisions?"

> "My religion is simple. My religion is kindness."
>
> —THE DALAI LAMA

Several years ago, I stumbled onto an idea that is as controversial as it is obvious. I had already concluded that grace was a far more central concept in religious faith than was routinely acknowledged in the churches I attended. Indeed, in my religious tradition, grace was out of favor. It was common, among our leaders, to negate even God's grace with the word "but." Someone would intone, "Yes, I know we are saved by God's grace, but . . . ." After the "but" could come any number of words, concepts, rules, or restrictions that essentially eliminated God's grace for anyone who did not believe or act in a particular way.

Yes, we believe in the grace of God, *but* you have to adhere to correct doctrine . . . *but* you have to attend church regularly . . . *but* you have to be against abortions and homosexuals . . . *but* you have to tithe . . . *but* whatever you do, it will never be good enough. You began to get the idea that such people were happy with the thought that certain people would not bother them on the streets of Paradise.

These legalists are not limited to any one faith or denomination. You can find them in Baptist churches, Jewish synagogues, Muslim mosques, and Roman Catholic cathedrals. In fact, you can find them as the treasurer or keeper of the purse or constitution in Rotary clubs, garden clubs, school boards, and the United States Senate.

The controversial aspect of my discovery was that Judas, after his betrayal of Jesus, went to the wrong people looking for grace. Judas's story is in the Bible, but, as many times as I have read the story of the Passion of Christ, I had never seen the following facet before: in the Gospel of St. Matthew, after Jesus is arrested and tried, Judas goes to the religious leaders and attempts to undo his betrayal of Jesus. He even gives the money back, making restitution. The Bible, depending on which translation you read, says Judas repented, had remorse, and/or regretted his action. The trouble is that he went to the wrong people looking for grace! What if he had gone to Jesus and asked for forgiveness? Would he have been forgiven? I believe he would have!

More than 2,000 years have passed, and little has changed. There are religious leaders, churches, synagogues, mosques, even entire "Christian" denominations who have forgotten they are in the grace business!

Laws are usually helpful, and they exist for good reasons. However, as every person who has tried to overcome silly laws or traditions has discovered, there exists a cadre of individuals who see their primary task as protecting the traditions! They will smile at you and tell you they love you as they pull the trigger, thinking they have done their god and you a favor.

Every faith tradition with a holy book, whether the Koran or the Book of Mormon, the Hebrew Scriptures or the Christian Bible, has enough words that can be read to justify as much death and destruction as you are inclined to undertake. If you don't want to kill people, there is still the possibility of making them miserable and treating them unkindly in God's name (or Allah's name, Buddha's name, Yahweh's name, or Jehovah's name). They may say they are doing this "for your own good." That is sometimes true when they are responsible for protecting children.

> "For true love is inexhaustible; the more you give, the more you have."
>
> —ANTOINE DE SAINT-EXUPERY

But to treat other adults as incompetent, unable to make their own decisions, is rarely a kindness. It is difficult to justify treating anyone with hostility or contempt or vengeance as a loving act.

Someone told me that if something feels like a punch in the stomach, then it probably is! As a rational adult, if you do not want to be bothered by me, even though I have the cure for cancer in a bottle and the keys to paradise in a book, then loving action seems to require that I leave you alone. There are exceptions when an "intervention" is indicated, but be careful. That is, be full of care. Be full of grace. The word "love," alone and without context, can become useless and meaningless.

## MegaLove

The next massive snag, when we try to understand love, has to do with corporate behavior as contrasted with individual behavior. Reinhold Niebuhr wrote the classic text on this topic, *Moral Man and Immoral Society* (New York/London: C. Scribner's Sons, 1932). Organizations and states do not have the capacity to love. An individual can make decisions counter to his or her own instincts for survival. I can choose to do what is best for you instead of acting in my self-interest. Parents do this all the time. Husbands and wives also act selflessly many times in the course of their marriages. Sometimes children behave nobly in caring for their parents. Occasionally, a stranger risks life and limb to save someone in danger. Such are the stories of our heroes and heroines and saints.

According to Niebuhr, clubs, associations, churches, societies, denominations, unions, businesses, corporations, other organizations and institutions, nations, and states will not, except on the rarest of occasions, act selflessly. In the greatest irony, they would often rather die than act compassionately.

Where are the leaders who ask the question, "What is the right thing to do?" As governments and industries and institutions make poor decision after poor decision with regard to the environment, the poorest and most marginalized members of our societies, health care, our international relationships, and hundreds of other issues, we just plow ahead based on the momentum of the past, taking care of our business, playing partisan politics, and being indifferent to real people and their real problems.

No country or cartel is alone in its misbehavior. Bad decisions are routine in international affairs. I recently heard a general interviewed on NPR about the hostilities of the Middle East. Speaking of the ethnic battles within Iraq, he said, "Nothing will change until they decide they love their children more than they hate their neighbors."

Amen to that.

# Appendix

## A. "All about You" Script Analysis

Script analysis is not an exact science. There are not ten magic questions guaranteed to reveal your deepest reasons for your most embedded and embarrassing lifelong habits. We are more complicated than that. But answering certain questions can give us clues to the way we think and why we do the things we do. I recommend that you write your answers to these questions in a journal, then read my commentary that follows each one. These are typical of questions many therapists would ask you.

1. What is your *name*? Do you have nicknames? Who named you? Which of those names did you like and which did you dislike? Did you ever make an effort to change the name by which you were/are known?

Why are questions about names important? Your name was not an accident. Your parents carefully chose it for a purpose. If they were casual, or careless, about the selection of your name, that too is important. Were you valuable enough for them to invest a bit of thought in the first thing people would know about you, your "label," your moniker?

Were you named after a rich uncle? Does that say something about what they hoped for you financially? Did they give you one name from each grandmother? Does that say something about their sense of fair play, which they wanted to pass on to you? Did you name you after a pet? After a politician? After a comic book character? Who chose the name and why did they choose it? Because it was cute? Because it was powerful? What were their feelings about the name and what expectations came along with the name? Did they give you a name that "places" you ethnically? Did they give you a biblical name? Did your mother name you like a young girl names her toy doll? Was she still a child emotionally, playing "pretend," when she had you? Rarely are names unimportant. Something was going on in the household into which you were born. Can you determine what it was? What clues does your name give about who they wanted you to be? Aristocratic? Scholarly? An athlete? Southern? Italian? African American? Christian? Muslim?

Names often hint at the fantasy your parents have for your life. Sometimes a primary life script is implied in the name a person is given. The parent who names a child Pollyanna, Sunshine, or Happy is potentially setting a child on a different life journey than that of a child whose parents named (and called) him Einstein, Socrates, or Homer. One name is not necessarily better than the other, but you can be sure that those parents had different expectations of their children.

Nicknames you have had and what you have done with them are also important. They can be clues to who you were perceived to be and how you fit into your family of origin or into the community of your childhood. Junior, Sweetie, Bozo, Fatty, Prissy, Sis, Little Ralph, or a myriad other names could have implications that need to be examined. Do they tell you something about what your parents or teachers or coaches or friends expected from you? Or about what they didn't expect from you? This is the time to explore your hunches. Think about which nicknames stuck and which did not, and why. Even if your parents did not assign you the nickname, what was in the environment of your home and family circle that let the name stick so that, even as an adult, you recall it? In many families, every child has an assignment: Crazy Larry is the wild child. Plato is the bookworm. Tomboy Tommie is going to be the athlete, whether she wants to or not! What did your names or nicknames set you up to be?

> "In recovery, we learn to accept the darker side of ourselves. In family of origin work, we learn to accept the darker side of our parents too."
>
> —MELODY BEATTIE, *BEYOND CODEPENDENCY*

Sometimes, when people cannot live up to their names, they rebel. They go in the opposite direction from what their parents intended. Parents named a child Socrates, but he dropped out of school in the tenth grade. Why? Were the lofty standards unrealistic?

Think about whether you liked or disliked your names and nicknames. Did you change your name or nickname along the way? That can indicate that you wanted something different than what your parents planned for you, which may be a positive sign. If you decided you were no longer going to be Little Billy but rather function as an adult Bill or William, that is probably positive. If you abhor the pet name by which you are called, yet continue to tolerate it, then maybe a name change is one way you can grow up and assert your independence. If your father named you after his favorite bird dog Sam, and you have always resented the indignity of being named after an animal, you can alter your moniker. Your dad may always call you Sam, but your other family and friends who care about you and your feelings will work with you through a time of transition.

The goal is simply to understand, as best as you are able, what went on when you were named and what has been going on with regard to your various "labels" in the years since then.

2. What do you know about your *conception and birth*? Was there anything extraordinary, painful, wonderful, or otherwise significant about any part of your conception, your mother's pregnancy, labor, or delivery? Was any trauma involved? Were you wanted or unwanted?

Why are questions about your birth significant? Almost everybody has some sort of "birth story." Family myths about your birth actually can cover a wide range of time, from prior to your conception to well after you were delivered. Were your parents expecting you when they married? Did they get pregnant with you the day before your father went off to war? I know a person who was born nine months to the day after a house fire that killed her parents' first child. I always had the impression that she felt more like a replacement child than a person in her own right. Did the parents regret such a hasty pregnancy? They ended up divorcing. If known, the narrative of the events surrounding your conception can be instructive.

The same is true of the duration and difficulty of the pregnancy. Were you an easy pregnancy or a challenging one? What about your delivery? Was it trouble-free or traumatic? As consequential as the tangible events (the facts) is the attitude of your parents. If you were born in a taxi on the way to the hospital, do your parents treat that reality lightheartedly or solemnly? Did your early arrival make them say of you, "You never know where Sissi will show up next. She's a delightful free spirit." Or did they say, with somber seriousness, "Sissi has been a nuisance since the day she was born. She has always been a problem." The interpretation of the various episodes can be more significant than the actual events.

Everyone has a pedigree. You may not be born into royalty or the Boston Blue Book, but you were not born into a vacuum. Your history and your lineage matter! Discovering your birth myths can be one of the most pleasant and meaningful components of your pilgrimage into maturity. Use this subject as an excuse to ask your parents questions. Some parents are delighted to share their memories. Others, for reasons that may be significant, might resist. Do a bit of detective work. Ask other individuals—aunts, uncles, or older siblings—to help you piece together the events. What was going on in the world? War? In your family? Poverty? Travel? Couch your questions as oral history, and you will be doing a favor not only for yourself but for your children and grandchildren.

It is always within your power to reinterpret any of the scripts you were given. If your birth story is that you were born on the day of a terrible national tragedy, and that fact has always been used as a predictor that your life was somehow a bad omen, that pain follows you wherever you go, you can change that perception. Visit the library (or Google) to discover alternate events that occurred on the same date. Thousands, millions of things happen daily. Why not choose some of the good activities and change your birth story: "Do you know what other great thing happened on the day I was born?"

3. Describe *your parents* when you were a child. Were they happy or depressed? Was life in your family a constant fight or was it peaceful? Was it boring? Describe your parents' marriage. Describe how they treated you. How did that compare to how they treated your siblings? What was the best thing about your parents? What was the worst thing about your parents?

4. Describe *other relatives who were important in your family*: brothers and sisters, aunt(s), uncle(s), grandparent(s), or others (even if unrelated) who lived with you for a period of time or to whom you were especially close. What was the best thing about each person? What was wrong with each person?

Why is information about your immediate family vital to understand? Nothing and nobody is more crucial in the creation of your personality than your parents. If they were going through a bitter divorce, that affected you. If they were perfectionists, that made a difference in you. If they were sloppy housekeepers, that made its mark on you. Whoever they were, whatever they did or didn't do, you are one of the consequences.

Of course, there were other influences. If Dad abandoned the family, then Grandma or Granddad may have had a more significant impact. Even so, Dad's absence was momentous. A nanny or a next-door neighbor may have functioned as a parental surrogate, affecting your life greatly. Nonetheless, you worked out some mythology in your childhood mind to explain your reality. Stories such as Cinderella are less fairy tales than fidelity tales; it is an act of your childhood psyche working out a reasonable justification and allowing you to be faithful to your birth parents.

Most of us had one or two parents present, and they were influential. We learned our primary feeling scripts from them: "Do this" and "Don't do that." Whether they were doting parents who spoiled us or angry parents who belittled us, we are primarily the product of what we learned from them—the spoken and the unspoken lessons.

As you explore your memories about your parents, you will be surprised to learn that your siblings do not necessarily have the same recollections: "Mother would have never said that!" That difference in your memories should not be surprising since you were not raised in exactly the same family as your siblings! There is almost always one favored and one less blessed child in the clan. One daughter may have gone through adolescence when Dad was drinking heavily, and the other when Dad was sober and going to AA meetings every night. Every offspring does not have the same IQ or the same talents or the same friends outside the family, and those differences meant that each sibling is treated differently. Parents ordinarily have higher expectations of the oldest child, which is why so many presidents are oldest sons. Young men are usually raised and socialized differently than young women, for good and ill. No two people have ever been raised in exactly the same family. Even with twins, one is known to be older than the other and treated differently, with the rights and responsibilities of the firstborn withheld from the younger twin. Also, the smallest differences may be emphasized to distinguish between the two. Because of a few random, early cases of colic, Hilda starts to be known as the sweet child and Tilda as the one with a temper. But once the behavior is named, it is looked for and expected. The parents begin to treat Hilda as the charming child she is becoming, and Tilda is designated the strong-willed twin.

> "You may give them your love but not your thoughts, for they have their own thoughts. You may house their bodies, but not their souls."
>
> —KAHLIL GIBRAN,
> *THE PROPHET*

Some issues, however, are not subtle. If your parents were on welfare for your entire childhood, there will be differences in how you were raised than if your parents were multimillionaires. Saints can come from either kind of household. So can child-batterers. Any set of parents can teach their children that they are worthless or that they are priceless. The goal before us is not to stress over the past but to understand it. What did it feel like to be in your family?

As a counselor, I have met resistance from some people about delving into family history: "Why do you want to know all this stuff about my aunts and uncles? What does that have to do with the fact that my husband is having an affair?" Good question. The answer is, "Maybe nothing." The answer could also be, "Maybe a lot." We are trying to understand our family scripts. What goes on in our individual lives that is directly traceable to our peculiar family dynamics? This is not always easy to identify. If I were counseling you in my office, I would be looking for the "Aha!" moment, the explanation when you sigh or nod your head and say, "Yeah, that makes sense." To get there, you may have to explore several options that you reject.

As an example, I want to be clear that if your husband is having an affair, you are not responsible for his affair. Let's start there. Neither is your mother, father, aunt, or uncle. Exploring family stories may, however, give you clues about why certain emotions are felt and decisions are made. For example, how your family and how your husband's family dealt with sexual matters can be instructive. Also, how your family and how your husband's family dealt with conflict can be enlightening. Did he always "win," and did you always "lose"? If your husband functioned as the "favored child" in his family system, enjoying a sense of entitlement (he always got what he wanted), and you functioned as the "caretaking" or "peacemaking" sibling, always taking what was left over emotionally in your household, then you and your husband may have brought your family scripts from childhood directly into your marriage—he gets what he wants when he wants it, and you submit to his whims. Understanding such processes can help you know what you need to change. If you don't change your self-understanding and your way of relating to "entitled" men, then even if you get a divorce, you are likely to find a second husband (and maybe a third and fourth) who "complement" your need to be a caretaker or even a victim. Your husband may be the "guilty" party, but there are still lessons you can learn about yourself and how you relate to him and to others.

5. Name your *family traditions*. Are there any family stories or unusual events (these might go back several generations)? Is any ancestor well known, for good or ill? What did your family do on holidays?

6. What is your *earliest childhood memory*? Where did you live? With whom? Was there any kind of crisis in your family life when you were a child?

7. When you were in grade school, what was your *favorite summer activity*?

8. What was your *favorite childhood game*? What was your *favorite childhood book or story*? What *subjects* did you enjoy in school? What did you enjoy doing away from school? What was your *favorite song* as an adolescent? Who were your *heroes and heroines*? What was your *favorite holiday*? What was your *hobby*?

9. Describe a *typical family meal*. Who sat where at the table? Who cooked? Who cleaned? What were your favorite meals?

10. If you could *change one thing* about your childhood and adolescence, what would it be?

Why do these random questions about your childhood provide insight into your adult personality? Preadolescence is when you began to have independent input into becoming who you became. Parents could introduce you to various games, from Monopoly to Scrabble to soccer, but they could not force you to like one of those more than bridge or baseball. You began to choose which of their trademark characteristics you would embrace, which you would modify, and which you would reject.

Some of your life scripts come directly from how much you bought into your parents' choices, and how much you decided to go your own way. If your family opened Christmas presents on Christmas Eve rather than Christmas morning, and now, as an adult, you do the same, then that is a family script you have adopted. It is neither good nor evil, but it is now yours! If your new spouse had a family script of opening presents on Christmas Day and *never* on Christmas Eve, then the two of you are headed inexorably for your first holiday conflict.

Family traditions are remembered for a reason. Some basis existed to rehearse certain behaviors. Maybe your family remembers the story of Great-grandpa Smith's night in the woods at the moonshiner's still. It is a fabulous saga, and everyone laughs when it is told. But, like everyone else, you had eight great-grandparents. Why is only one "family story" remembered, while the narratives of the other seven are forgotten and lost to history? Each one of them had a thousand stories. Why were they not recalled at family get-togethers? Why was that one particular story part of family lore? Ask questions of other family members. What was important about the woods? What about the moonshine still? What does that particular yarn evoke that is part of an important family pattern? The woods on the family farm? Alcohol? Maybe nothing . . . maybe a lot.

When a skilled therapist asks these questions, he or she can follow up with additional questions that help uncover family scripts. Not every answer is important. Maybe the story about the still in the woods is just a humorous tall tale and nothing more. Maybe your favorite song was your favorite because you could sing along with it and not because it had a deep symbolic meaning. But maybe it did. Have someone help you sort through your answers to discard what is unimportant and attend to what is useful. My favorite songs were "Puppy Love" and "Rockin' Robin," and if there is a profound lesson to be learned from either of those, I still don't know what it is.

> "Much of the work of psychotherapy consists of attempting to help our patients allow or make their response systems more flexible."
>
> —SCOTT PECK,
> THE ROAD LESS TRAVELED

But my favorite book as a youngster was *Robinson Crusoe*. As I began to understand some of the things that make me tick, it makes perfect sense that I was enchanted by the idea of being alone on a tropical island, not having to entertain anyone, relate to anyone, or interact with anyone. When you are as obsessively gregarious as I am, then time away from people sounds appealing. Even as a twelve-year-old, more than two decades before I went to therapy, my soul and my spirit were responding to the psychic pain of too much talking and trying to find a healing solitude. Being alone on an isolated island seemed desirable to me.

Maybe your earliest childhood memory is of your parents arguing. My earliest recollection is being in church. Given my profession, do you think that is important? I do.

What you did with your time is a clue to who you were and who you are! If you were involved in competitive sports every afternoon, every weekend, and every summer, do you think that is a clue to who you were and who you became?

If your mom cooked all the meals and your dad came home late from work every day, don't you suppose those images imprinted on you? Mothers are cooks and fathers work late. I am not assigning value judgments to your childhood experiences. They were what they were. But you should be aware that if you thought a woman's place was in the kitchen, then that notion will be with you until you die unless you rewrite that script. You may be happy with that script, or you may not be. Which behaviors do you see as peculiar? Which do you see as the norm? Right now, we are merely exploring the origins of our habits. Where did this conduct start?

11. There are probably certain sentences that you could finish if your mom or dad (or primary caregiver) began to say them. Fill in the blanks as if that person were speaking:

Don't ever _____.
You are incapable of _____.
You should always _____.
You have no choice about _____.
Life is _____.
Be _____.

Why are these fill-in-the-blank statements important? These imperatives tell you some of the primary scripts within your family system. If you look in a thesaurus for "imperative," you will read synonyms such as "requirement," "essential," "rule," "necessity," "obligation," and "law." These are the "musts" and "shoulds" of your household. These are the tasks that duty either required or made taboo in your home. You may have heard your parents or their substitutes say such sentences a thousand times. Even if they never said these words exactly, most of us know how our parents would have finished these all-encompassing, comprehensive attitudes about life. Consider these as well:

a. All men _____.
b. Never trust anyone who is _____.
c. Money is good for _____.
d. Always pay attention to _____.
e. In our family, women should _____.

f. Sex is _____.
g. You will go to hell if you _____.
h. At least once a week you should _____.

You get the idea. How you fill in the blanks of such statements indicates what you were taught as a youngster—your scripts. Even if your parents or other caregivers never actually said these particular sentences, this exercise helps you understand the intense emotions that are part of every household. Paul Carlson calls these "primary feeling scripts." In uncovering your scripts, you will look (in your memory) for sentences from your mother and father (and/or your most significant caregiver) that start with the word "be" or the phrase "you are." For every person who assumes every child is told, "You are beautiful and wonderful," there is another who is equally certain that every child receives the message, "You are a mistake, a pain, and a bother." The challenge is to be honest enough with yourself to determine the real messages in your family.

What you have remembered reflects how your mother and father felt about themselves. If your mother (or mother substitute) was an overweight woman, she may have told you to "clean your plate." If your dad was competitive, he may have encouraged you to be an excelling athlete. What were the messages from your earliest infancy that you heard repeatedly in actual words or in actions?

Also, what were the things your parents told you not to do? Again, pretend you are six years old, or age ten or twelve. What do you hear your parents prohibiting, large or small? "Don't" messages are as important as "do" messages in analyzing your childhood scripts. And they may be easier to remember!

We are trying to uncover some of the negative feelings in your family. What made your parents uptight? What were they afraid of? Most people don't want to look bad in public. In your family, how did that play out? Did it matter to your parents where you went to school? Or that you were taught how to sew? Or that you could "drink like a man"? Some families don't want to offend God. Some families don't ever mention God. You can choose to go in a different direction than your family, but your baseline, your default position is to function as you were taught to function, to speak the same literal language and to live out of the same cultural customs.

As you attempt to remember the idiosyncrasies of your particular family and childhood, more memories are better than less. Write down the short phrases that were common in your family experience, especially from your mother and your father.

Everyone's experience in your family was not identical. In your family system, there may have been a belief (either stated or underground) that boys are smarter than (or more responsible than or tougher than) girls. Therefore, boys in your family may have gotten the message, "Be a leader" and "Speak up," while girls may have gotten the message, "Be submissive" or "Be quiet." The oldest son may have gotten the message, "You are the heir to the family fortune," and the daughters may have been told, "Be pretty and marry well." You need to discover the messages you received from your mother and father in your family. Those life scripts facilitated you in becoming you. Your scripts are as unique as your DNA, the amazing combination of characteristics that belong to you and you alone. Unlike your DNA, however, you can change your life scripts!

In one family, older siblings may have been taught, "Don't trust anybody." Younger children, born after some life-altering experience in the pilgrimage of the parents, were coached differently: "Do trust people." No two people grew up in the same family. I was a different parent to my second child than I was to my first. I had more money. I had less patience. Furthermore, my youngest child, nine years younger than my oldest, grew up with three big people (Mom, Dad, and big sister) in her world, whereas my oldest had only two big people (Mom and Dad) in her family. We were the same biological parents for both girls, but we provided them different family experiences.

12. How have people in your family died? How do you *expect to die?* At what age?

Why are these questions about death necessary? Surprisingly, we are capable of scripting even how and when we die. If you have ever heard, "The men in our family die young," there may be a physiological cause, but there may also be a psychological basis. Both the body and the spirit may be involved! If you have decided you will probably die young anyway, it does not require a PhD in psychiatry to know that some self-fulfilling tendencies might also be at work—you smoke cigarettes and eat pork barbeque and warm chocolate cake with scoops of ice cream with regularity because, well, why not? You expect to die young anyway!

Also, there are lifestyles that simply do not lend themselves to a lengthy life expectancy. If I am counseling someone who already has a couple of drunk-driving arrests, honest self-reflection on this question will lead to the conclusion that a car wreck is a likely cause of death. Simply naming the reality can be helpful.

- "If I continue to get in bar fights, then I could die in a bar fight."
- "If I continue to have unprotected, promiscuous sex, then I am likely to catch AIDS."
- "If I continue to avoid the doctor, even when I need a doctor, then I am likely to die prematurely from a treatable illness.

This last "bullet" is another reminder of how scripts work. Many men have been taught that men aren't supposed to be sick, that only girls and "sissies" or hypochondriacs get sick or go to the doctor. That kind of attitude was not imprinted on anyone's DNA at birth. It is learned behavior; therefore, it was taught behavior: "Suck it up and go." "No pain, no gain." "Don't be a wuss."

Those may be perfectly fine admonitions for a tenth grade boy (or girl) trying to make the high school basketball team, but they are foolish life scripts for a fifty-year-old man with a lingering and unexplained skin rash and/or growth on his body. Our scripts affect not only our lives but also our deaths.

13. What is your greatest disappointment in life thus far? What is your greatest success? What do you think you will be doing ten years from now if things go badly? What do you think you will be doing ten years from now if things go well?

Why are these questions about your past accomplishments and failures and your future expectations noteworthy? The best predictor of the future is the past. Naming the past, its failures and its victories, is crucial to the possibility of change. My friend Ted Godfrey hands out a business card that reads, "Keep on doing what you have always done, and you will get what you have always gotten." A variation of the same theme (I have seen this attributed to Albert Einstein) defines insanity as doing the same thing over and over and over again and expecting different results.

When I work with churches that are between pastors, I lead them through a three-step process. I ask them to "dust off the trophy case" (My Baptist colleague, John Lepper's phrase) and review what they have already accomplished in their rich heritage. What about their early years do they brag about? What were their successes? I get them to tell me about their best traditions, what makes them proud about their past. Then I move them to the present: What do they like about their church now? What makes them feel satisfied when they drive into the parking lot or enter the building or meet their friends or give their tithe? Next, I encourage them to think about their future—their short-term outlook (two years) and their long-term potential. What are their expectations? What are their opportunities? What are their challenges?

> "There are years that ask questions and years that answer."
>
> —Zora Neale Hurston

Men and women who pay consultants thousands of dollars to help them ask and answer those questions in their businesses never seem to ask or resolve those same uncertainties in their personal lives. If my business is successful, it will accomplish certain goals, make a specific amount of money, move into new markets, create new widgets, whatever. But ask those same shrewd entrepreneurs what they intend to do with their marriages, their families, and their own hopes and dreams, and they have no idea what you are talking about! Are there trips they want to take, sights they wish to see, relationships they desire to improve, projects they yearn to achieve, and legacies they want to leave? They appear never to have thought of that! They can boost the annual bottom line at the office by two percent, but they can't figure out how to spend two weeks of vacation per year with their families, or even watch two nights of television per week with their teenagers.

Most people in counseling can describe their negative scenario fairly easily. It usually involves a dead marriage, destroyed family relationships, unemployment, disease, and/or death. But they struggle to articulate what they desire. I have a list on my computer labeled "Vacation Fantasies," places I would like to visit. I love moving locations from my "To Do" list to my "Done" list. Last year I checked the following off my list: whale watching (off the New England coast), the Cape Cod Baseball League (the nation's premier college wooden bat league), Wounded Knee (on the Pine Ridge

Reservation in South Dakota), and Brazil (my first trip ever to South America).

Those aren't the only trips I took. I was also able to go to four countries in eastern Europe, but honesty compels me to admit they weren't on my "To Do" list. More significant than travel, I always want to spend time with my family. I have begun to take my grandson fishing, even though children his age don't have long attention spans. I want to have "quality time" with my daughter who lives down the block, with my daughter who recently moved out of state, and with my wife who lives in the same house, the same bedroom, and the same bed as me! I also have goals regarding the completion of this volume and beginning to prepare for retirement. Not much happens "naturally." Planning and effort are required.

Ten years from the time I write this paragraph, I will be one month short of seventy years old. I hope to be retired, in excellent health, able to spend time with family, able to write more, and able to afford to travel. Most importantly, as a Christian person, I want to continue to make a positive difference in the lives of the destitute, the depressed, and the disenfranchised of the world. I even have a plan for that. I have heard that retirees who stop working without a new job or a significant hobby die or go crazy within two years of their retirement. I have seen evidence that this may be true.

14. What would you like to give yourself *permission* to do?

Why is this question about "permission" important? Most of us will not do what we believe is forbidden or taboo. Taboos are not limited to extreme activity, such as incest. If you will not get a divorce because "no one in our family has ever gotten a divorce," then you have discovered one of your family's taboos. If you say, "I don't believe in spending money foolishly," then you have named a taboo. If there were no taboos for you for the next few years, nothing prohibited, nothing unacceptable, what would you do differently?

"I'm not crazy.
I'm just not you."
(OVERHEARD)

If there are laws against the items on your "wish list," then you are bumping up against a genuine social taboo. You are not allowed to murder your spouse or steal from your employer. But many of our taboos are merely unexamined family and cultural scripts. Find yourself some new possibilities. Consider these:

- Fifty-year-old men can change careers.
- You are allowed to "shop for" a new friend.
- A wife does not have to put up with her husband's abuse.
- You can go back to school.
- You are not required to be afraid of everything you were taught to be afraid of.
- An adult child of an alcoholic can quit rescuing her/his parent.
- You can buy a better house in a better neighborhood.
- You can change religions.
- You are allowed to say "No."
- You are allowed to say "Yes."
- Emotionally healthy people can go to counseling. Indeed, that may be an indication of improving mental health. The person who needs assistance but refuses to get aid is the one in trouble!
- You can lose weight.
- You can quit worrying about your child who is on the verge of failing out of school and stop protecting him/her from the consequences of that decision.

What would you like to give yourself permission to do? To release? To start? To stop? Most of what we think is unacceptable, sometimes even unmentionable, is perfectly normal and done every day by good people. If you need a friend, pastor, rabbi, counselor, or coach to help you determine the difference in illegal and immoral behavior as opposed to prohibitions that are merely family or cultural scripts, then secure someone's assistance. If you need a partner to walk with you and encourage you, then find someone, even if you have to pay that person, who will do just that. Life is too short to keep doing what makes you and everyone else miserable. Don't delay. Help yourself. Get help.

## B. More about God

God deserves more than an appendix. But since God gets such bad press, I thought it best to ease into this conversation about "spirituality" as gently as possible. Given some of the promoters who market their understanding of God, I appreciate the reluctance of those who refuse to buy. A lot of mean, inflexible, shameless, unloving, uncaring,

> "The first step to wisdom is the fear of the Lord."
>
> —PROVERBS 9:10

even evil people seem to be in the god business. They would gladly kill for Jesus' sake. They would happily jihad for Mohammed's sake. They would cheerfully maim for Buddha or Vishnu.

> "If God is for us, who can be against us?"
>
> —ROMANS 8:31

Still stuck with what they were taught "once upon a time" about the Almighty, they have no room for growth or change in their comprehension of the Incomprehensible. Someone, somewhere and sometime in their lives, gave them definitions of the One Who Is Mysterious (the Hebrew name for God is "I AM WHO I AM"), and those designations and prescriptions worked for that particular time and place in ordering their lives:

- Obey these Ten Commandments and you will be a good person.
- Believe these Five Fundamental Articles of Faith and you will be a true believer.
- Pray six times a day facing east and you will be pious.
- Take a pilgrimage to this sacred shrine and you will be more holy.
- Make these sacrifices (of money, of family, of time) and you will be virtuous.

The trouble with living by rules, even grand and comprehensive commandments that seem God-given, is that there are always exceptions, the need to nuance. The Ten Commandments (in Exodus 20) of the Hebrew Bible demonstrate the dilemma. "Thou shalt not kill" seems straightforward and universal. The difficulty is that the next twenty chapters of Exodus are, at least partially, a treatise on when it is appropriate to kill—for example, when to impose the death penalty and when to go to war. It turns out that there are degrees and distinctions to what at first appeared to be an inviolate decree. Interpreting or translating the Hebrews words as "Thou shalt not murder" is merely another way to nuance. What exactly does that imperative, that prohibition, mean?

Individuals who are stuck, who do not grow, believe they have God figured out and feel (genuinely) that it is their duty to God and to you to get

> "That God has managed to survive the inanities of the religions that do him homage is truly a miraculous proof of his existence."
>
> —BEN HECHT

you on the right side of God by any means possible, no matter how much it demeans or even destroys you. They figure it is better for you *to lose your life and to save your soul.*

However, that last phrase is one more example of bad religion being substituted for a helpful or healthy faith. In this instance, the words of Jesus are misrepresented. Jesus (recorded in Matthew 16:26) did say we have made a bad decision if we exchange our souls for the material goods of this world. But that choice is an individual decision. The worthiness or destiny of my soul is not in your mortal and fallible hands. I am willing to submit to the edicts and verdicts of Almighty God, but not to you.

My Christian faith tells me that a merciful God is my Advocate.

The temptation is to create God in our own image. People who are angry are partial to an angry god, and people who are sweet and good-natured are fond of a deity with a kinder disposition. White folks create a blue-eyed Jesus, and black Africans, in their art, give Jesus dark skin, dark hair, and dark eyes. Poor people believe God cares especially for the poor, and many of the rich believe their wealth is a sign that God has blessed them, that they more perfectly reflect God than others.

One way to think about who and what your gods are is to examine your checkbook and your calendar. For what do you spend your money? On what do you spend your time? Which relationships, which hobbies, which people, which activities get the majority of your money and time?

Maybe we do build our gods to suit us. No one is purely objective. As I have gotten older, I have observed that many people who name the same God that I name, the

> "It is a mistake to suppose that God is only, or even chiefly, concerned with religion."
>
> —WILLIAM TEMPLE, ARCHBISHOP OF CANTERBURY

> "Religion can be the enemy of God. It's often what happens when God, like Elvis, has left the building. A list of instructions where there was once conviction; dogma where once people just did it; a congregation led by a man where once they were led by the Holy Spirit."
>
> —BONO

God of the Judeo-Christian tradition, think differently than I do about God. We read the same holy book, the Bible, but we end up worshiping and living differently. Monogamists, polygamists, and celibates defend their lifestyles using the Bible. People who consume alcoholic beverages and those who abstain attribute their behavior to Holy Scripture.

God sends mixed messages. Is the truly pious convert to be a quiet contemplative or an aggressive activist? I can make a case for each from the Bible, and I suspect the same is true for most other faith traditions. Is God close by or far away or both? Which is more important: love or justice? grace or law? Is true faith conserving or liberating? Is it sometimes a bit of each? The Bible does not speak with one clear voice on most subjects, which is why the Presbyterians can emphasize predestination and the Methodists can accentuate free will.

Because we are human, religious debates tend to be little different from controversies about land or sex or money or power. Some fight with a "winner takes all" mentality. Rather than encouraging individual faithfulness to God, some zealots would obliterate any residue of unbelief by force—even if slaughter and destruction are required. Then we are back again to the problem of creating our gods in our own image, or even worse, making ourselves into God, the Righteous Judge, which is the biblical definition of blasphemy.

Of course, you don't have to be even remotely religious to play this game. Every tavern in town has more than its fair share

> "If God is great and God is good, then why is your heaven so small?"
>
> —SUSAN WARNER

of the self-righteous and proud. There is no need to get too judgmental about church folks. They may be no better than the population at large, but they are surely no worse. And I would like to make a case that over the centuries, maybe people of genuine faith in God have done more good, on the whole, than harm. In addition to the millions of small acts of charity that will never be known or reported anywhere, many of the great advances in human evolution, from medical breakthroughs to improved civil liberties are directly attributable to an individual's religious convictions.

One of the most interesting courses I took during my seminary career was called "Cults." The textbook was horrible. We studied a variety of religious groups that most Christians would consider heretical or unorthodox. The textbook was little more than a brief description about each of the supposedly offensive belief systems—a short history of their worst blunders: Mary Baker Eddy's marriages, Joseph Smith's inconsistencies, in-fighting and power struggles of the Jehovah's Witnesses, *ad nauseum*. Even a cursory course in logic will teach you that an idea cannot be disproved because of the misbehavior of the person who had the idea. And a superficial study of the Christian church will show you that we have a few thousand years of our own foolishness we would need to defend: inquisitions, crusades, witch hunts, church splits, *ad nauseum*.

My goal is not to defend God or to attack those who do not believe in God, but merely to testify, "I believe." If there is a God, and I believe there is, what I say about God probably matters less than what God says about me.

> "I worship God as Truth only. I have not yet found Him, but I am seeking after Him. I am prepared to sacrifice the things dearest to me in pursuit of this quest. Even if the sacrifice demanded my very life, I hope I may be prepared to give it."
>
> —MAHATMA GANDHI

Still, here are some of my summary thoughts about God:

1. God loves us and is on our side.
2. We are to love God.
3. We are to love others and ourselves.
4. We are to listen to the many ways in which God speaks.
5. Listen more and talk less.
6. We all make mistakes and fail.
7. God's grace had better be the last word, or we are all in trouble. (The law is good but never good enough.)
8. Life is a school where we learn how to trust God.
9. Fear not.
10. Repent. Change. Adjust.
11. Assume/accept responsibility when you are responsible.
12. Be open.

This book may contain more about me and more about God than you want to know, but I hope it will help you learn more about yourself than you have ever known. May your pilgrimage through the remainder of your life be a fascinating, enriching, and joyful pilgrimage.

"What we are is God's gift to us. What we become is our gift to God."

—ELEANOR POWELL

Made in the USA
Charleston, SC
25 August 2013